Typescript for Front End Development

Reduce Errors, Boost Productivity, and Master Modern Web Development Like a Pro

Adriam Miller

2

3

Discover Other Books in the Series

"TypeScript for Beginners: A Beginner's Guide to the Future of JavaScript"

"TypeScript for Backend Development: Backend applications with Node.js, Express, and modern frameworks"

"TypeScript for Blockchain: Unlock the full potential of TypeScript in Web3 development"

"TypeScript for DevOps: The Secret Weapon for Automating, Scaling, and Securing Your Infrastructure"

"TypeScript for JavaScript Developers: The Essential Guide for JavaScript Developers to Write Safer, Scalable, and More Efficient Code"

"Typescript for Microservices: Learn How to Leverage TypeScript to Develop Robust, Maintainable, and Efficient Microservices Architecture"

"TypeScript for Mobile Application Development: Build Faster, Safer, and Smarter Applications with Ease"

"TypeScript for Web Development: Boost Your Productivity, Eliminate Costly Errors, and Build Scalable Web Applications with TypeScript"

For more information, or to book an event, contact :
(Email & Website)

Book design by Adriam Miller
Cover design by Adriam Miller

Disclaimer

The information provided "**Typescript for Front End Development: Reduce Errors, Boost Productivity, and Master Modern Web Development Like a Pro**" **by Adriam** Miller is for educational and informational purposes only.

This Book is designed to provide insights into TypeScript programming and its applications in blockchain and Web3 development.

Introduction

Welcome to **"TypeScript for Front End Development: Minimize Errors, Enhance Productivity, and Excel in Modern Web Development."** In today's rapidly changing digital environment, the need for robust and scalable web applications has never been greater, prompting developers to increasingly adopt TypeScript as their preferred programming language. This book is designed to equip both experienced developers and those new to web development with the essential knowledge and tools to fully leverage TypeScript's capabilities.

TypeScript transcends being merely a superset of JavaScript; it represents a revolutionary technology that emphasizes type safety, superior tooling, and enhanced code clarity in front-end development. By utilizing TypeScript, developers can identify errors early in the development cycle, decrease debugging time, and ultimately produce cleaner, more maintainable code. This leads to a more efficient development process, allowing you to concentrate on creating high-quality applications that fulfill user expectations.

Throughout this book, we will explore the fundamental principles of TypeScript while examining its practical uses in front-end development. We will guide you through the essential components of the language, ranging from basic type annotations to advanced generics, and demonstrate how these concepts can be applied within popular frameworks such as React, Angular, and Vue.js. Each chapter is structured to build upon the previous one, facilitating your journey from grasping the basics to mastering more intricate subjects.

In addition to learning the syntax, this guide will offer best practices and strategies for effectively incorporating TypeScript into real-world projects. You will learn how to work with existing JavaScript codebases and transition to TypeScript gradually, ensuring a seamless integration without interrupting your workflow. Furthermore, we will discuss key tools and features that TypeScript provides, including interfaces, enums, and decorators, empowering you to write more efficient and contemporary code.

As you embark on this journey, keep in mind that the world of web development is constantly changing. New tools, frameworks, and methodologies emerge regularly, and staying current is crucial for success. With TypeScript, you are not only investing in a language but also equipping yourself with a skill set that will enhance your career and make you a more adaptable developer.

Join us as we explore the powerful capabilities of TypeScript and unlock new opportunities for creativity and efficiency in front-end development. It's time to reduce errors, boost productivity, and master modern web development like a pro! Let's get started on this exciting journey together.

Chapter 1: Introduction to Typescript for Front End

JavaScript has established itself as a fundamental component of front-end development, demonstrating its versatility and strength as a programming language. Nevertheless, as web applications have evolved in complexity, many developers have faced challenges that require a more sophisticated coding approach. This is where TypeScript becomes relevant.

TypeScript, created by Microsoft, is a statically typed superset of JavaScript that offers a variety of features aimed at enhancing the development experience, improving code quality, and ensuring maintainability. By incorporating type checking and advanced tooling, TypeScript enables developers to identify errors early in the development cycle and promotes better collaboration among team members.

1.1 What is TypeScript?

TypeScript is frequently referred to as JavaScript with type annotations, a description that effectively encapsulates its core attributes. It builds on the principles of JavaScript while introducing static typing and contemporary programming paradigms. As a superset of JavaScript, any valid JavaScript code is also valid in TypeScript, allowing developers to gradually transition to TypeScript and take advantage of its features without the need to overhaul their entire codebase.

Notable features of TypeScript include:

Static Typing: By permitting developers to specify types, TypeScript facilitates the detection of type-related

9

errors during development rather than at runtime.

Enhanced IDE Support: TypeScript offers improved autocompletion, refactoring capabilities, and inline documentation in modern integrated development environments (IDEs), simplifying the process of writing and comprehending code for developers.

Improved Readability and Maintainability: Well-defined types and interfaces clarify the intended use of variables, functions, and objects, resulting in code that is more self-explanatory.**Advanced Features**: TypeScript supports modern JavaScript features, such as async/await, destructuring, and arrow functions, as well as additional features like enums, decorators, and interfaces that help manage complex codebases.

1.2 Why Use TypeScript for Front-End Development?

Front-end applications have grown increasingly intricate, necessitating a structured approach to development that promotes scalable and maintainable code. Here are a few compelling reasons to consider TypeScript for your next front-end project:

Early Error Detection: With its static type system, TypeScript allows developers to catch errors at compile-time rather than runtime. This early detection can save significant debugging time and improve the overall quality of the code.

Better Team Collaboration: TypeScript's type annotations facilitate clearer communication among team members. When different developers work on a shared codebase, the explicit types serve as contracts that define how different parts of the application interact.

Seamless Integration with JavaScript Frameworks: TypeScript works effectively with popular front- end frameworks like React, Angular, and Vue.js. Each of these frameworks has embraced TypeScript, and using it can lead to enhanced performance and reduced bugs in component-based architectures.

Community and Ecosystem: TypeScript enjoys a vibrant and active community, which means a wealth of resources, libraries, and integrations are readily available. The growing adoption of TypeScript in the industry further solidifies its relevance and robustness.

1.3 Getting Started with TypeScript

For developers already familiar with JavaScript, transitioning to TypeScript can be straightforward. Below are the fundamental steps to get started with TypeScript in a front-end project:

Installation: Begin by installing TypeScript through npm. In your project directory, you can run:

```bash
npm install typescript --save-dev
```

Configuration: Create a `tsconfig.json` file for your project, which will define the compiler options and project structure for TypeScript. A simple configuration might look like this:

```json
{
"compilerOptions":    {   "target":   "es6",   "module":
```

"commonjs", "strict": true, "esModuleInterop": true

},

"include": ["src/**/*"],

"exclude": ["node_modules", "**/*.spec.ts"]

}

```
```

Writing TypeScript: Start writing TypeScript files with a `.ts` extension instead of `.js`. For example, you could create a simple function with type annotations:

```typescript
function greet(name: string): string { return `Hello, ${name}!`;
}
console.log(greet("World"));
```

Compiling TypeScript: Run the TypeScript compiler to convert your TypeScript files into plain JavaScript:

```bash npx tsc
```

Integrate with Front-End Frameworks: Explore the documentation of the front-end framework you are using to understand how to incorporate TypeScript effectively. Most popular frameworks provide guides on setting up TypeScript within their ecosystems.

As web applications grow more complex and demanding, the need for a structured and maintainable approach to front-end development becomes increasingly critical. TypeScript offers a powerful solution by enhancing JavaScript with static typing and improved tooling. Embracing TypeScript not only helps to write safer code but also fosters better collaboration and readability within teams.

Understanding TypeScript for Front End Development

Originally developed by Microsoft, TypeScript is a superset of JavaScript that adds static typing and other features, making it an attractive choice for developers focused on front-end development. In this chapter, we will explore the fundamentals of TypeScript, its advantages over traditional JavaScript, and practical examples of its usage in front-end projects.

What is TypeScript?

TypeScript is an open-source programming language that builds on top of JavaScript by adding optional static typing, interfaces, and other powerful features. This means that it allows developers to write code that can be checked for errors during development, rather than at runtime, which can dramatically improve code quality and maintainability.

Static Typing

The most significant advantage of TypeScript is its static typing capability. While JavaScript allows for dynamic typing—which provides great flexibility—it can also lead to various types of runtime errors. By contrast, TypeScript enables developers to define types explicitly, which can help catch errors early in the development process. For instance:

```typescript
let message: string = "Hello, TypeScript!";

message = 42; // This line will raise a compile-time error
```

This feature ensures that the variable `message` is expected to hold a string value, providing immediate feedback if improper assignments are made.

Enhanced Tooling and IDE Support

TypeScript's static typing allows for better tooling and IDE support, enhancing developer productivity. Integrated Development Environments (IDEs) such as Visual Studio Code provide advanced features like autocompletion, type inference, and quick fixes, making the coding experience smoother. This means that as developers type, they receive real-time feedback and suggestions, reducing the likelihood of mistakes and the time spent debugging.

Interoperability with JavaScript

Another compelling aspect of TypeScript is its complete interoperability with JavaScript. Developers can incrementally adopt TypeScript in existing JavaScript projects. You can rename a `.js` file to `.ts` and start adding types, or even leave parts of your code in JavaScript. This flexibility is crucial for teams looking to gradually transition to TypeScript without the need for a complete rewrite.

Benefits of Using TypeScript in Front-End

Development ### Improved Code Quality By enforcing type checks and providing interfaces and type definitions, TypeScript improves code quality. It helps developers write cleaner, more predictable code by encouraging them to think about data structures and function definitions. This leads to fewer bugs and easier maintenance.

Scalability

As projects grow in size and complexity, maintaining a JavaScript codebase can become increasingly challenging. TypeScript helps manage this complexity through its modular approach, interfaces, and advanced features, enabling teams to work more effectively on larger codebases. This is particularly beneficial for large teams where multiple developers are working on the same code.

Enhanced Collaboration

TypeScript creates a shared understanding of the codebase. With clear type definitions and interfaces, developers can collaborate more effectively, as the intended usage of functions and classes is explicitly defined. It becomes easier for new team members to understand the codebase, reducing the onboarding time and improving overall team efficiency.

Getting Started with TypeScript

Starting with TypeScript is straightforward. Here are some steps to help you begin your journey: ### 1. Installing TypeScript

You can install TypeScript via npm (Node Package Manager) with the following command:

```bash
```

npm install -g typescript
```

### 2. Compiling TypeScript

TypeScript files are usually saved with a `.ts` extension. Once you write your TypeScript code, you need to compile it into plain JavaScript. This can be done via the following command:

```bash tsc app.ts
```

This command generates a `app.js` file that can be executed in any environment that supports JavaScript.
3. Configuring TypeScript

To manage your TypeScript project more effectively, you can create a `tsconfig.json` file in the root directory of your project. This configuration file allows you to specify compiler options, include/exclude files, and define other settings that suit your project requirements. A simple `tsconfig.json` may look like this:

```json
{
"compilerOptions": { "target": "es6", "module": "commonjs", "strict": true, "esModuleInterop": true
},
"include": ["src/**/*"]
}
```
```

4. Writing Your First TypeScript Application

Let's create a simple TypeScript application that takes user input and displays a greeting. Here's a sample implementation:

```typescript
function greet(name: string): string {
return `Hello, ${name}! Welcome to TypeScript.`;
}
const userInput: string = "Alice";
console.log(greet(userInput));
```

Compilation

You would compile this code the same way as before with the `tsc` command, resulting in a `greet.js` file. ### 5. Integrating TypeScript with Frameworks

TypeScript has excellent integration with popular front-end frameworks such as Angular, React, and Vue. For instance, when building a React application with TypeScript, developers can use type annotations for props and state management, which enhances code clarity and reduces runtime errors. Most modern frameworks provide TypeScript templates and configurations to help you get started easily.

By embracing TypeScript, you can elevate your coding practices, reduce errors, and improve collaboration within your team. As we move further into the age of TypeScript, understanding its practical applications will become increasingly essential for any front-end developer.

Setting Up TypeScript: Installation, Compiler, and Configuration

The improved tooling, better developer experience, and the ability to catch errors at compile-time make TypeScript an excellent choice for modern software development. This chapter outlines the essential steps to set up TypeScript, covering installation, compiling TypeScript code, and how to effectively configure it to suit your project's needs.

1. Installation

Before we dive into using TypeScript, we need to install it on our machine. TypeScript can be installed in several ways, depending on your project setup and preferences.

1.1 Installing Node.js

TypeScript relies on Node.js for its installation and execution. Therefore, ensure you have Node.js installed. You can download and install Node.js from nodejs.org. To verify your installation, run the following command in your terminal:

```bash
node -v
```

You should see the version number displayed. ### 1.2 Installing TypeScript Globally

Once Node.js is installed, you can install TypeScript globally using npm (Node Package Manager), which comes with Node.js:

```bash
npm install -g typescript
```

The `-g` flag installs TypeScript globally so you can access the `tsc` command from any directory. After installation, verify your TypeScript installation by running:

```bash
tsc -v
```

This command should display the installed version of TypeScript. ### 1.3 Installing TypeScript Locally

In many cases, you may want to install TypeScript locally within a specific project. This way, you ensure that your project uses a specific version of TypeScript regardless of the global installation. To do this, navigate to your project folder and run:

```bash
npm install --save-dev typescript
```

Using `--save-dev` indicates that TypeScript is a development dependency. After installing, you can check the `devDependencies` in your `package.json` file.

2. Compiler

Once TypeScript is installed, you will use the TypeScript compiler, commonly referred to as `tsc`, to compile

TypeScript files into JavaScript. The compiler converts TypeScript code, which may contain types and other language features not available in JavaScript, into plain JavaScript that can run in any JavaScript environment.

2.1 Compiling a TypeScript File

To compile a TypeScript file, first create a file with a `.ts` extension, such as `example.ts`. You can write some simple TypeScript code:

```typescript
function greet(person: string) { return `Hello, ${person}!`;
}
let user = "Jane Doe"; console.log(greet(user));
```

To compile this TypeScript file into JavaScript, run the following command in your terminal:

```bash
tsc example.ts
```

This will generate a corresponding `example.js` file in the same directory, containing the compiled JavaScript code:

```javascript
function greet(person) {
return "Hello, " + person + "!";
}
var user = "Jane Doe"; console.log(greet(user));
```

```
```

2.2 Using `tsconfig.json`

In larger projects, manually compiling individual files can quickly become cumbersome. TypeScript provides a configuration file called `tsconfig.json` that specifies the root files and the compiler options required to compile the project.

To create a `tsconfig.json` file, you can run this command in your project directory:

```bash tsc --init
```

This command generates a `tsconfig.json` file with a default configuration, which you can customize according to your project's needs.

3. Configuration

The `tsconfig.json` file contains various options that dictate how TypeScript behaves. Here are some common options you might want to consider:

compilerOptions: This section allows you to specify various options that affect the compilation process. Some important options include:

`"target"`: Specifies the ECMAScript target version (e.g., `ES5`, `ES6`, `ESNext`).

`"module"`: Determines the module system to use (e.g., `CommonJS`, `ESNext`).

`"strict"`: Enables all strict type-checking options

21

(recommended for better type safety).

`"outDir"`: Specifies the output directory for the compiled JavaScript files.

`"rootDir"`: Specifies the root directory of your input files. Here's an example of a `tsconfig.json` file with common settings:

```json
{

"compilerOptions": { "target": "ES6", "module": "CommonJS", "strict": true,

"outDir": "./dist",

"rootDir": "./src"

},

"include": ["src/**/*"],

"exclude": ["node_modules", "**/*.spec.ts"]

}
```

3.1 Running the Compiler with Configuration

With a proper configuration in place, you can simply run `tsc` in the terminal, and it will read the configuration from `tsconfig.json` to compile all TypeScript files specified in the `include` field while respecting the options defined in `compilerOptions`.

3.2 Watching for Changes

TypeScript provides a watch mode that recompiles your files whenever changes are detected. To enable this, run:

```bash
tsc --watch
```

This command keeps the TypeScript compiler running in the background, allowing you to see changes in real-time as you develop your application.

We discussed how to install TypeScript both globally and locally, compile TypeScript files into JavaScript, and configure the TypeScript compiler using a `tsconfig.json` file. Setting up TypeScript correctly lays the foundation for robust development, enabling you to harness the full potential of the language with features like static typing, interfaces, and more. In the following chapters, we will delve deeper into TypeScript's features and best practices to help you write cleaner, more maintainable code.

Chapter 2: TypeScript Fundamentals

In this chapter, we will examine the essential principles of TypeScript, enabling you to grasp its benefits and how it can be utilized effectively in your projects.

What is TypeScript?

TypeScript, created by Microsoft, is tailored for the development of large-scale applications. In contrast to JavaScript, which is dynamically typed, TypeScript implements type checking at compile time. This feature allows developers to specify types for variables, function parameters, return values, and more, resulting in a more seamless development process by minimizing runtime errors and enhancing code quality.

Benefits of TypeScript

Static Typing: TypeScript identifies errors during the compilation phase rather than at runtime, facilitating the detection of issues prior to application deployment.

Enhanced IDE Support: Numerous code editors offer superior autocompletion, navigation, and refactoring capabilities when utilizing TypeScript, which can greatly enhance productivity.

Improved Code Readability: The incorporation of types and interfaces aids developers in comprehending the code more easily, which is particularly advantageous in collaborative environments.**Compatibility with JavaScript**: As a superset of JavaScript, any valid JavaScript code is also valid TypeScript code. This allows developers to gradually adopt TypeScript in existing JavaScript codebases.

Better Tooling: TypeScript comes with powerful tooling options, including integration with build systems, linters, and frameworks, providing developers with a robust development experience.

Getting Started with TypeScript

To begin using TypeScript, you need to install it in your development environment. You can do this via npm, the Node.js package manager:

```bash
npm install -g typescript
```

After installation, you can check that TypeScript is installed correctly by running:

```bash
tsc -v
```

This command will display the version of TypeScript installed on your machine. ### Writing Your First TypeScript Program

Let's start with a simple TypeScript program. Create a new file called `hello.ts` and add the following code:

```typescript
const greeting: string = "Hello, TypeScript!";

console.log(greeting);
```

In this example, we declare a variable `greeting` with a type annotation specifying that it is a `string`. To compile

25

this TypeScript file into JavaScript, you would run:
```bash
tsc hello.ts
```

This command generates a JavaScript file called `hello.js`, which can be executed in any JavaScript environment (like Node.js or a web browser).

Type Annotations

TypeScript allows you to explicitly specify the types of variables and function parameters. Here are some basic type annotations:

Number: Represents numeric value.

String: Represents text.

Boolean: Represents true or false.

Array: Represents a list of values.

Tuple: A fixed-size array with restricted types.

Enum: A way to define named numerical constants.

Any: A fallback type that disables type checking (use with caution). Example of using various type annotations:

```typescript
let age: number = 25;
let name: string = "Alice"; let isActive: boolean = true;
let hobbies: string[] = ["reading", "hiking", "coding"]; let user: [number, string] = [1, "Bob"]; // Tuple
enum Color { Red, Green, Blue } let myColor: Color =
```

Color.Red;
```
```

Interfaces

Interfaces are a powerful feature in TypeScript that allow you to define the shape of objects. They provide a way to enforce a specific structure on objects, ensuring that they have certain properties and methods.

Example of using an interface:

```typescript
interface Person {
name: string; age: number;
}
function greet(person: Person) {
console.log(`Hello, my name is ${person.name} and I am ${person.age} years old.`);
}
const personObject: Person = { name: "Alice", age: 30 };
greet(personObject);
```

In this example, the `Person` interface defines a structure that includes `name` and `age`. The `greet` function expects an argument of type `Person`, ensuring that any object passed to it meets the defined structure.

Functions

TypeScript also allows you to type function parameters and return values, enhancing function reliability. Here's an example:

````typescript
function add(x: number, y: number): number { return x +
y;
}

const result: number = add(5, 10); console.log(result); //
Output: 15
````

In this function, `x` and `y` are typed as `number`, and the function's return type is also specified as

`number`.

We have introduced you to the fundamentals of TypeScript, explaining its advantages, how to set up the environment, and key features like type annotations and interfaces. As you become more comfortable with these concepts, you'll find that TypeScript can significantly improve your productivity and the maintainability of your code.

Mastering Primitive and Complex Types (Strings, Numbers, Objects, etc.)

Understanding primitive and complex types is fundamental for any TypeScript developer, as it allows for writing more predictable and maintainable code. This chapter will cover the various primitive and complex types in TypeScript, including strings, numbers, objects, arrays, tuples, and enums.

1. Understanding Primitive Types

Primitive types in TypeScript are the most basic data types and include:

String

Number

Boolean

Null

Undefined

Symbol (introduced in ES6) ### 1.1 String

Strings in TypeScript can be defined using single quotes, double quotes, or backticks (for template literals). Here's how to work with strings:

```typescript
let firstName: string = "John"; let lastName: string = 'Doe';

let fullName: string = `${firstName} ${lastName}`; // Template literal console.log(fullName); // Output: John Doe
```

1.2 Number

All numeric values in TypeScript are of type `number`, including both integers and floating-point values.

```typescript
let integer: number = 42; let float: number = 3.14;

let hexadecimal: number = 0x00FF; // Hexadecimal console.log(float); // Output: 3.14
```

1.3 Boolean

The Boolean type represents a logical entity that can have two values: `true` or `false`.

```typescript
let isActive: boolean = true;

let hasPermission: boolean = false;
```

1.4 Null and Undefined

By default, `null` and `undefined` are subtypes of all types. You can explicitly declare variables to accept these types:

```typescript
let nullableValue: null = null;

let undefinedValue: undefined = undefined;
```

1.5 Symbol

The Symbol type is used to create unique identifiers for object properties. It is primarily used when you want to avoid name clashes.

```typescript
let uniqueId: symbol = Symbol('id');
```

Summary of Primitive Types

TypeScript provides an excellent range of primitive types that are useful for declaring simple data. Understanding these types is crucial for effective type annotation and ensuring the reliability of your code base.

2. Exploring Complex Types

While primitive types are foundational, complex types are constructed from primitive types and are more powerful for building sophisticated data structures.

2.1 Objects

Objects are collections of key-value pairs and can represent more complex data. You can define an object type using an interface or inline:

Defining Objects Using Inline Types:

```typescript
let user: { name: string; age: number } = { name: "Alice", age: 30 };
```

Using Interfaces:

```typescript
interface User {
name: string; age: number;
}
let user: User = { name: "Alice", age: 30 };
```

2.2 Arrays

Arrays are collections of similar types. You can define an array in TypeScript using two syntaxes:

```typescript
```

```
let numbers: number[] = [1, 2, 3, 4, 5];
let strings: Array<string> = ["apple", "banana", "cherry"];
```

2.3 Tuples

Tuples allow you to create arrays with fixed sizes and specified types for each element.

```typescript
let tuple: [string, number] = ["John", 25];
console.log(tuple[0]);    //    Output:    John
console.log(tuple[1]); // Output: 25
```

2.4 Enums

Enums are a way to define a set of named constants, helping to create meaningful labels for numeric values, improving code readability.

```typescript enum Direction {
Up = 1,

Down, Left, Right,

}

let move: Direction = Direction.Up; console.log(move); //
Output: 1
```

2.5 Any and Unknown Types

The `any` type allows you to opt out of type-checking, which can be counterproductive in larger applications. Instead, the `unknown` type is a safer alternative, allowing only limited operations until you assert its actual type.

```typescript
let dynamicValue: any = "this can be any type";
dynamicValue = 42; // Valid assignment

let uncertainValue: unknown = "this can also be any type";

// let valueString: string = uncertainValue; // Error: Type 'unknown' is not assignable to type 'string'

// Type assertion
if (typeof uncertainValue === "string") {

let valueString: string = uncertainValue; // Now it's valid

}
```

By leveraging TypeScript's type system, developers can catch errors at compile time rather than at run time, leading to more reliable programs.

Type Inference, Type Annotations, and Type Assertions

One of the core features that TypeScript offers is the ability to infer types, specify type annotations, and utilize type assertions. This chapter delves into these three important concepts, exploring their functionality and how they contribute to effective TypeScript programming.

1. Type Inference

1.1 What is Type Inference?

Type inference is a powerful feature of TypeScript where the compiler automatically deduces the type of a variable or expression based on its value or usage context. This means that developers do not always need to explicitly define types, as TypeScript can understand the intended type from the assigned value.

1.2 How Type Inference Works Let's consider a simple example:

```typescript
let greeting = "Hello, World!";
```

In this case, TypeScript infers the type of `greeting` to be `string` because a string value is assigned. This automatic detection enhances code readability and reduces the verbosity of type declarations.

Type inference is not limited to variable declarations. It is also applicable in function return types, function parameters, and more complex structures like arrays and objects.

1.3 Different Levels of Type Inference TypeScript applies several levels of inference:

Local Inference: This occurs when TypeScript can determine the type from a single expression. The example provided earlier is an illustration of local inference.

Contextual Typing: When a function takes a parameter, TypeScript can infer the type based on the expected structure of the parameter. For instance:

```typescript
window.onmousedown = function(mouseEvent) {
console.log(mouseEvent.button); // Type of mouseEvent is inferred to be MouseEvent
};
```

Generics and Inference: TypeScript can also infer types in generic functions or classes, allowing flexibility while maintaining type safety.

2. Type Annotations

2.1 What are Type Annotations?

Type annotations explicitly specify the type of a variable, function parameter, return value, or object property. They provide clarity and ensure that the values assigned meet the expected structure. Using type annotations is particularly helpful in complex codebases where implicit types may lead to errors.

2.2 Using Type Annotations

Type annotations are added by appending a colon followed by the type after a variable declaration. Here are some examples:

```typescript
let age: number = 25;
let userName: string = "Alice"; let isActive: boolean = true;
```

In addition to basic types, TypeScript supports more complex types, such as arrays, tuples, and even custom types created through interfaces and types.

2.3 Annotating Function Types

Type annotations can also be applied to function parameter and return types. For example:

```typescript
function add(x: number, y: number): number { return x +
y;
}
```

In this function, TypeScript knows that both `x` and `y` must be numbers and that the function will return a number.

2.4 Benefits of Type Annotations

The use of type annotations provides the following benefits:

Clarity: They make the code easier to read and understand.

Type Safety: They help catch errors at compile time rather than run time.

Enhanced IDE Support: Many IDEs leverage type information for autocompletion and error checking. ## 3. Type Assertions

3.1 What are Type Assertions?

Type assertions give developers the ability to specify or "assert" a more specific type for a variable than the compiler inferred. It tells the TypeScript compiler to treat an entity as a different type. Type assertions can be particularly useful when developers have more context about a value than TypeScript can infer.

3.2 Using Type Assertions

Type assertions utilize the `as` keyword or angle bracket syntax. Here's an example:

```typescript
let myValue: any = "This is a string";

let strLength: number = (myValue as string).length;

// Alternatively

let strLength2: number = (<string>myValue).length;
```

In both cases, we assert that `myValue` is of type `string`, thereby allowing us to access properties and methods associated with strings.

3.3 When to Use Type Assertions

Type assertions should be used judiciously. They bypass TypeScript's type checking, so it's crucial to ensure that the asserted type is correct. Common scenarios for using type assertions include:

When working with data retrieved from external sources where the type is known.

When interfacing with legacy JavaScript code.

When needing to clarify the type of a complex object.

By understanding how to leverage these tools, one can

37

maximize the benefits of TypeScript, leading to more maintainable and reliable applications. As you continue your journey with TypeScript, becoming adept in these areas will facilitate better code quality and developer productivity.

Chapter 3: Interfaces and Type Aliases

This chapter explores these two fundamental concepts, how they differ, and when to use each effectively. ## 3.1 Understanding Interfaces

3.1.1 What is an Interface?

In TypeScript, an interface is a syntactical contract that an entity should conform to. Interfaces define the structure of an object, including its properties and methods, without specifying how they should be implemented. This abstraction allows for designing flexible and reusable components.

```typescript interface User {
id: number; name: string;

email?: string; // optional property age?: number; // optional property greet(): string; // method declaration
}
```

In the example above, the `User` interface declares a structure that includes the properties `id`, `name`,

`email`, and `age`, as well as a method `greet`. The properties `email` and `age` are optional, indicated by the question mark (`?`).

3.1.2 Implementing Interfaces

Classes can implement interfaces, providing their own specific implementations of the defined properties and methods.

```typescript

```

```typescript
class Person implements User { constructor(
public id: number, public name: string, public email?:
string, public age?: number
) {}
greet(): string {
return `Hello, my name is ${this.name}.`;
}
}
const user = new Person(1, "Alice", "alice@example.com",
30); console.log(user.greet()); // Output: Hello, my name
is Alice.
```

The `Person` class implements the `User` interface,
adhering to its contract by defining the required
properties and methods.

3.1.3 Extending Interfaces

One of the powerful features of interfaces is that they can
be extended, allowing for the creation of more complex
types by inheriting properties from existing interfaces.

```typescript
interface Admin extends User { role: string;
}
const admin: Admin = { id: 2,
name: "Bob",
email: "bob@example.com", role: "administrator",
```

```
  greet: () => `Hello, I am ${this.name}, your ${this.role}.`
};
console.log(admin.greet()); // Output: Hello, I am Bob,
your administrator.
```

Here, the `Admin` interface extends `User`, adding a new
`role` property. Any object of type `Admin` must satisfy
the structure defined by both interfaces.

3.2 Understanding Type Aliases ### 3.2.1 What is a
Type Alias?

A type alias in TypeScript is a name given to a specific
type. This can include primitive types, union types, or
more complex structures, but type aliases do not create a
new type; instead, they provide a better way to refer to
existing types.

```typescript
type UserID = number; type UserEmail = string;
```

Type aliases can also represent object types, making them
similar to interfaces.

```typescript
type UserProfile = { id: UserID;
name: string; email?: UserEmail; age?: number;
};
```

3.2.2 Using Type Aliases

41

Type aliases can be very useful when dealing with complex types, especially when using union types or when combining multiple types.

```typescript
type ID = number | string;
let userId: ID;
userId = 101; // valid
userId = "ABC123"; // also valid
```

In this example, `ID` can be either a `number` or a `string`, enhancing flexibility. ### 3.2.3 Type Aliases vs. Interfaces

While interfaces and type aliases can often be used interchangeably, some key differences exist:

Extensibility:

Interfaces can be extended using the `extends` keyword, and they can also merge declarations with the same name (declaration merging).

Type aliases cannot be extended in the same way and do not support declaration merging.

Use Cases:

Use interfaces when designing a contract for objects, especially when creating APIs or libraries where you want to specify how objects should behave.

Use type aliases when you need to define complex types, unions, or intersections.

Consistency:

Interfaces are always open for extension; type aliases are closed. ### 3.2.4 Example of Type Aliases

```typescript
type Point = {
x: number; y: number;
};
type Circle = Point & { radius: number;
};
const circle: Circle = { x: 0,
y: 0,
radius: 5
};
```

In the above example, `Circle` is defined as an intersection type merging `Point` and its additional property

`radius`. This demonstrates how type aliases can create complex structures.

By allowing for clear definitions of types, these constructs aid in enhancing type safety and facilitating better communication about expected structures within your code.

Creating and Extending Interfaces for Scalable Code

In this chapter, we will delve into creating and extending interfaces, showcasing best practices and patterns that enhance the maintainability and scalability of your code.

Understanding Interfaces

An interface in TypeScript is a syntactical contract that an entity must conform to. It's a powerful feature that allows you to enforce the shape of an object, ensuring that it has specific properties with defined types.

Basic Interface Definition

To define an interface, you use the `interface` keyword. For example:

```typescript
interface User {
id: number; name: string; email: string;
}
```

This `User` interface describes an object with three properties: `id`, `name`, and `email`. Any object that conforms to this interface must contain these properties, adhering to their respective types.

Implementing Interfaces

Once you have an interface defined, you can implement it in a class:

```typescript
class UserProfile implements User { constructor(
```

```typescript
public id: number, public name: string, public email:
string
) {}
}

const user1 = new UserProfile(1, "John Doe",
"john@example.com");
```

In this snippet, the `UserProfile` class implements the `User` interface, ensuring that any instance of

`UserProfile` will fulfill the contract specified by `User`.
Creating Extensible Interfaces

Extensibility is crucial for maintaining a scalable codebase. TypeScript interfaces support inheritance, allowing you to build upon existing interfaces without modifying them directly. This is particularly useful when working with a large application where changes can have far-reaching effects.

Extending Interfaces

You can create a new interface that inherits from an existing one using the `extends` keyword:

```typescript
interface Admin extends User { role: string;
}
const adminUser: Admin = { id: 2,

name: "Jane Smith",

email: "jane@example.com", role: "Administrator"
```

```
};
```

In this example, the `Admin` interface extends the `User` interface, adding an additional `role` property. This way, you can create specialized versions of existing interfaces without duplicating code.

Multiple Interface Inheritance

TypeScript also supports the implementation of multiple interfaces in a class. This allows for greater flexibility when defining complex objects:

```typescript
interface Contact {

phone: string; address: string;

}

class AdminUser implements User, Contact { constructor(

public id: number, public name: string, public email: string, public phone: string, public address: string

) {}

}

const adminDetails = new AdminUser(3, "Alice Brown", "alice@example.com", "123-456-7890", "123 Admin St, City");
```

Here, the `AdminUser` class implements both the `User` and `Contact` interfaces, ensuring it has both the properties from each contract.

Leveraging Indexable Types

In addition to defined properties, you might want to create interfaces that allow for dynamic property names. TypeScript's indexable types can help with this scenario.

Defining Indexable Interfaces

You can define an indexable interface using a string index signature, which enables you to access properties dynamically:

```typescript
interface StringArray { [index: number]: string;
}
let myArray: StringArray = ["Hello", "World"];
```

In this example, `StringArray` allows you to create an array-like structure where each index corresponds to a string.

Practical Scenarios for Extending Interfaces ### API Responses

Suppose you are working with an API that returns user data. You could define a base interface for common user attributes and extend it for specific API responses:

```typescript
interface BaseUser {
id: number; name: string; email: string;
}
interface ApiResponseUser extends BaseUser { createdAt: Date;
updatedAt: Date;
```

47

```
}
```
```
```

In this scenario, expanding your `BaseUser` interface allows you to cleanly manage variations of data structures while keeping your codebase organized.

Component Props

In a React application, you can define your components using interfaces and then extend them for more specialized components:

```typescript
interface ButtonProps { label: string;
```
```typescript
onClick: () => void;
}
```
```typescript
interface IconButtonProps extends ButtonProps { icon: string;
}
```
```typescript
// Usage
```
```typescript
const IconButton: React.FC<IconButtonProps> = ({ label, onClick, icon }) => (
```

```
<button onClick={onClick}>
```
```
<img src={icon} alt="" />
```
```
{label}
```
```
</button>
```
```
);
```

```
```

This allows you to maintain a clear interface for the button while extending it to include additional properties for specific cases (like an icon), promoting reusability.

By understanding how to create basic interfaces, implement them in classes, extend them for more specific use cases, and leverage indexable types, you empower yourself to build applications that are both maintainable and scalable.

Type Aliases vs Interfaces: Key Differences and Best Practices

While they might seem similar at first glance, they have distinct characteristics and best practices that can impact the way we write robust and maintainable TypeScript code. This chapter aims to outline the key differences between type aliases and interfaces, explore their respective use cases, and provide best practices for implementing them effectively.

Understanding Type Aliases

A type alias in TypeScript allows developers to create a new name for an existing type. Type aliases can be defined for primitive types, unions, tuples, and even interfaces, enabling flexibility in type definitions.

Syntax

```typescript
typescript type User = {
name: string; age: number;
```

```
};
```

In this example, `User` is a type alias representing an object type with properties `name` (a string) and `age` (a number).

Features of Type Aliases

Flexibility with Unions and Intersections: Type aliases can represent any type, including unions and intersections:

```typescript
type Response = Success | Error; // Union type

type Admin = User & Permissions; // Intersection type
```

Ease of Use: Type aliases require less boilerplate than interfaces, making them concise and straightforward for simple types.

Serialization and Deserialization: Type aliases work seamlessly with libraries for data transformation, making them suitable for defining API responses.

Understanding Interfaces

An interface, on the other hand, serves as a contract that enforces structure on objects and classes. Interfaces are extensible, allowing developers to create more complex types and enhance existing ones.

Syntax

```typescript
typescript interface User {
```

```typescript
name: string;
age: number;
}
```

Here, `User` is an interface that describes an object with `name` and `age` properties. ### Features of Interfaces

Extensibility: Interfaces can be extended using the `extends` keyword, allowing developers to create new interfaces based on existing ones:

```typescript
interface Admin extends User { permissions: string[];
}
```

Declaration Merging: TypeScript's interfaces support declaration merging, which allows multiple declarations of the same name to combine into a single interface. This is particularly useful for augmenting third-party library types.

Implementation in Classes: Interfaces provide structure for class implementations, ensuring that classes adhere to contract definitions:

```typescript
class UserClass implements User { name: string;
age: number;
constructor(name: string, age: number) { this.name = name;
```

```
this.age = age;
}
}
```
` ` `

Key Differences Between Type Aliases and Interfaces

While type aliases and interfaces can often be used interchangeably, there are critical differences that developers should be aware of:

Extensibility:

Interfaces support extending and merging, enabling a more hierarchical design.

Type aliases do not support these features. Once defined, a type alias cannot be modified.

Basic Types:

Type aliases can define primitive types, unions, intersections, and tuples.

Interfaces can primarily define object structures and class contracts.

Declaration Merging:

Interfaces can merge declarations, which can lead to extending a type over time without breaking changes.

Type aliases cannot be merged; they produce an error if declared with the same name again.

Compatibility:

Both interfaces and type aliases can be used to create objects with the same shape, but `type` cannot be implemented by classes, whereas `interface` can.

Best Practices

When to Use Interfaces

Public API Definitions: Use interfaces when defining the shape of public APIs, especially when they may need to grow or evolve over time due to declaration merging.

Class Contracts: Prefer interfaces to define the structure that classes should follow, as they enforce a clear contract.

Complex Object Structures: Choose interfaces when you want to define comprehensive object communications, focusing on code readability and maintainability.

When to Use Type Aliases

Simple Types: Use type aliases for simple types or when defining union and intersection types. They provide a cleaner and less verbose way to represent complex data types.

Data Transformation: Opt for type aliases when you are dealing with transformations between different types, particularly in data manipulation or serialization.

Avoiding Merging Conflicts: Use type aliases in scenarios where declaration merging could lead to conflicts or where you want to prevent the unintentional extension of types.

While they may seem similar, using the right tool for the job can make your code more maintainable, readable, and adaptable to changes. By applying these principles, you can harness the power of TypeScript effectively and create robust TypeScript applications that are well-structured and easy to evolve. Ultimately, the choice between type aliases and interfaces should be guided by the specific requirements of your project and the architectural approach you wish to adopt.

Chapter 4: Generics for Reusable Code

TypeScript, a superset of JavaScript, enhances the language with static typing, and among its many features, generics stand out as a powerful tool for creating reusable code. This chapter explores generics in TypeScript—what they are, how they work, and how to implement them effectively for reusable code.

4.1 Understanding Generics

Generics allow developers to define flexible functions, classes, and interfaces that can operate with various data types while maintaining type safety. Instead of specifying a single type, generics enable us to use a placeholder, often represented by `T`, `U`, or other letters, to capture multiple data types in a single construct.

Why Use Generics?

Type Safety: Generics bring compile-time type checking, alerting developers to type mismatches early in the development process.

Reusability: By defining components that can work with different data types, generics promote code reuse, reducing duplication.

Readability and Maintenance: Code that clearly expresses its intent through generics makes it easier for developers to understand how to use it without sacrificing type information.

4.2 Basic Generics Syntax

To define a generic function, we introduce a type parameter inside angle brackets (`<T>`). Here's how to create a simple generic function:

```typescript
function identity<T>(arg: T): T { return arg;
}
let numberIdentity = identity<number>(42); // returns a number
let stringIdentity = identity<string>("Hello, Generics!");
// returns a string
```

In this example, the `identity` function takes an argument of type `T` and returns the same type. When calling the function, we can specify the type, but TypeScript is also smart enough to infer it from the argument provided.

4.3 Generics with Collections

Generics shine when dealing with data structures like arrays and lists. Instead of using the `any` type, which defeats the purpose of type safety, we can define arrays using generics.

```typescript
function getFirstElement<T>(arr: T[]): T | undefined {
return arr[0];
}
const firstNumber = getFirstElement<number>([1, 2, 3]);
// returns 1 const firstString = getFirstElement<string>(["a", "b", "c"]); // returns "a"
```

In this case, the `getFirstElement` function works with any array type while still ensuring that the return type matches the array's elements.

4.4 Generic Interfaces and Classes

Beyond functions, generics can also be implemented in interfaces and classes. This greatly increases their versatility.

Generic Interface

```typescript
interface Pair<K, V> { key: K;
value: V;
}
const numberStringPair: Pair<number, string> = { key: 1,
value: "One"
};
```

Generic Class

```typescript
class Box<T> {
private contents: T;
constructor(value: T) { this.contents = value;
}
getContents(): T { return this.contents;
}
}
const numberBox = new Box<number>(123);
console.log(numberBox.getContents()); // returns 123
```

```
```

In both examples, we utilize type parameters for flexibility, allowing our structures to accommodate varying types without losing type safety.

4.5 Constraints in Generics

Sometimes, it's useful to restrict the types that can be passed to a generic function or class. Constraints allow us to enforce specific characteristics on our generic type parameters.

```typescript
interface Lengthwise { length: number;
}

function logLength<T extends Lengthwise>(arg: T): void {
console.log(arg.length);
}

logLength({ length: 10 }); // Works

// logLength(123); // Error: Argument of type 'number' is
not assignable to parameter of type 'Lengthwise'.
```

In this snippet, the `logLength` function can only accept arguments conforming to `Lengthwise`, meaning any type passed must have a `.length` property.

4.6 Using Multiple Type Parameters

Generics in TypeScript also allow for multiple type parameters. This enables more complex scenarios where you need to work with more than one type.

58

```typescript
function merge<T, U>(first: T, second: U): T & U { return
{ ...first, ...second };
}

const mergedObject = merge({ name: "Alice" }, { age: 30
}); console.log(mergedObject); // { name: "Alice", age: 30
}
```

Here, the `merge` function takes two parameters of types
`T` and `U` and returns an object that combines both
types.

By leveraging generics, developers can fulfill the principle
of DRY (Don't Repeat Yourself) and build applications
that are not only robust but also adaptable to changing
requirements.

Introduction to Generics: Why They Matter in Front-End Development

One of the most powerful features of TypeScript that helps
in achieving these goals is generics.

Generics provide a way to create reusable components
that work with various data types while maintaining type
safety. They allow developers to write functions,
interfaces, and classes that are agnostic to the exact types
they operate on, promoting code reusability and reducing
duplication. By leveraging generics, developers can build
more flexible and maintainable codebases, which is
especially beneficial in front-end development.

The Value Proposition of Generics in Front-End Development

Type Safety: One of the primary reasons generics are valuable in front-end development is that they enhance type safety. With generics, developers can define a component or function that accepts values of a certain type without sacrificing the benefits of type checking. This reduces the likelihood of runtime errors, which are especially problematic in user-facing applications where a seamless user experience is crucial.

Code Reusability: Generics enable developers to create versatile components that can handle various data types. For instance, a generic data-fetching component can be written once and reused to fetch different kinds of data without code duplication. This reusability is essential in modern front-end frameworks like React, where building reusable components is a core principle.

Improved Maintainability: As teams evolve, applications grow, and codebases expand, maintaining code can become cumbersome. Generics facilitate the creation of modular and highly reusable code segments, making maintenance easier. When components are built with generics, modifications can often be made to one part of the code without affecting others, thus reducing the risk of introducing bugs.

API Design: In front-end development, API consumption is a common task. Using generics allows developers to create type-safe interfaces for handling responses from APIs. For example, when working with a RESTful service that may return various data models, generics can define a single interface that adapts to the response structure, ensuring accurate type checks and enhancing code readability.

Enhanced Collaboration: In a collaborative development environment, clear communication and understanding between team members are vital. Generics make it easier to articulate the intent of components and functions. When a component is defined with generics, its flexibility and the types it can accept are explicit, facilitating better teamwork and comprehension of the code.

Real-World Examples

Creating a Generic Component

Consider a simple example of a generic List component in a React application. Instead of hardcoding the types of items the List can take, we can define it to accept any type:

```typescript
import React from 'react';

interface ListProps<T> { items: T[];

renderItem: (item: T) => React.ReactNode;

}

const List = <T,>({ items, renderItem }: ListProps<T>) => { return (

<ul>

{items.map((item, index) => (

<li key={index}>{renderItem(item)}</li>

))}
```

```
</ul>
);
};
// Usage
const App = () => {
const numberItems = [1, 2, 3];
const stringItems = ['apple', 'banana', 'cherry'];
return (
<>
<List items={numberItems} renderItem={(item) =>
<span>{item}</span>} />
<List items={stringItems} renderItem={(item) =>
<strong>{item}</strong>} />
</>
);
};
export default App;
```
```

In this example, the `List` component is generic and can work with any type, be it numbers, strings, or custom objects. This example illustrates how generics enhance reusability and type safety.

### API Consumption with Generics

When consuming an API, we can define a generic fetch function:
```

```typescript
async function fetchData<T>(url: string): Promise<T> {
const response = await fetch(url);

if (!response.ok) {

throw new Error('Network response was not ok');

}

return response.json();

}

// Usage interface User { id: number; name: string;

}

async function getUserData() {

const          user          =          await
fetchData<User>('https://api.example.com/users/1');
console.log(user.name);

}
```

Using the generic `fetchData` function, we can fetch various types of data while ensuring that TypeScript checks the data structure returned from the API matches the expected format.

They empower developers to create type-safe, reusable, and maintainable components, which are crucial in building robust applications. As the web evolves, understanding and implementing generics can help developers manage complexity and improve collaboration, ultimately leading to more effective front-end development. Embracing generics is not just a good coding practice; it's a necessary skill for anyone seeking to excel in TypeScript and modern web development.

Advanced Generic Constraints and Utility Types

One of its powerful features is generics, which allows developers to create reusable components and functions that can work with any data type. In this chapter, we'll delve deeper into advanced generic constraints and utility types, exploring their significance in crafting flexible and type-safe applications.

1. Understanding Generics in TypeScript

Generics provide a way to create components that are not limited to a single data type but can work with multiple types instead. They facilitate code reusability, allowing developers to define functions, interfaces, and classes with type parameters.

Basic Generics

Let's start with a basic example of a generic function:

```typescript
function identity<T>(arg: T): T { return arg;
}
```

In this example, `T` is a type parameter that can be replaced with any type when the function is called. This enables `identity` to accept different types and return the same type, ensuring strong type-checking.

Creating Generic Interfaces

Generics are not limited to functions. You can also create generic interfaces:

```typescript
interface GenericBox<T> { value: T;
getValue: () => T;
}
const numberBox: GenericBox<number> = { value: 42,
getValue: () => numberBox.value,
};
const stringBox: GenericBox<string> = { value: "Hello,
TypeScript!",
getValue: () => stringBox.value,
};
```

Here, `GenericBox` can hold any type of value, making it highly reusable. ## 2. Advanced Generic Constraints

While generics are powerful, there are situations where you need to impose constraints on the types passed to them. This part covers how to use constraints effectively using the `extends` keyword.

Defining Constraints

You can restrict a generic type to ensure it meets certain conditions. For instance, if you want to create a function that only works with objects that have a `.length` property, you can define a constraint using an interface:

````typescript
interface Lengthwise { length: number;
}
function logLength<T extends Lengthwise>(arg: T): void {
console.log(`Length: ${arg.length}`);
}
logLength("Hello, World!"); // valid logLength([1, 2, 3]);
// valid
````

In this example, `T` must extend the `Lengthwise` interface, allowing `logLength` to accept any type that has a `length` property.

Combining Multiple Constraints

You can also combine multiple constraints by using intersection types. This allows you to require that a type satisfies multiple interfaces:

````typescript
interface Nameable {
name: string;
}
function greet<T extends Lengthwise & Nameable>(arg: T): void { console.log(`Hello, ${arg.name}. Length is ${arg.length}`);
}
greet({ name: 'Alice', length: 5 }); // valid
````

In this example, the generic type `T` must satisfy both the `Lengthwise` and `Nameable` interfaces, providing even tighter type safety.

3. Utility Types in TypeScript

Utility types are a set of widely used types in TypeScript that allow you to transform existing types in various ways. They are powerful tools to help you build complex types from simpler ones without repeating code.

Common Utility Types #### 3.1 `Partial<T>`

The `Partial<T>` utility type makes all properties in `T` optional.

```typescript
interface User {

id: number; name: string;

}

const updateUser = (userId: number, updatedUser: Partial<User>): void => {

// Implementation to update the user

};
```

With `Partial<User>`, you can pass an object that only has some of the `User` properties when updating. #### 3.2 `Pick<T, K>`

The `Pick<T, K>` utility type creates a type by picking a subset of properties from another type.

```typescript
```

```typescript
type UserPreview = Pick<User, 'name'>;
const preview: UserPreview = { name: "Alice"
};
```

Here, `UserPreview` only includes the `name` property, allowing you to create leaner types. #### 3.3 `Record<K, T>`

The `Record<K, T>` utility type creates an object type with keys of type `K` and values of type `T`.

```typescript
type UserRoles = Record<string, string>;
const roles: UserRoles = { admin: 'Administrator', user: 'Regular User'
};
```

In this example, `UserRoles` is a dictionary-like structure that maps roles to their corresponding descriptions. #### 3.4 `ReturnType<T>`

The `ReturnType<T>` utility type extracts the return type of a function type.

```typescript
type MyFunction = () => number;
type          ReturnTypeOfMyFunction          =
ReturnType<MyFunction>; // returns `number`
```

This is especially useful in scenarios where you need to use the return type of a function for other type definitions.

In this chapter, we explored the powerful combination of advanced generic constraints and utility types in TypeScript. Generics enhance the flexibility and reusability of your code by enabling type-safe abstractions. Meanwhile, utility types simplify type manipulation, allowing you to create intricate types with minimal effort.

Chapter 5: TypeScript with React

Using TypeScript with React enables us to write more robust and maintainable code, providing a set of powerful tools and features that help in catching errors early and improving code quality. This chapter will walk you through the key concepts and benefits of integrating TypeScript with React, how to set up your project, and how to leverage TypeScript's features in your React components.

5.1 Understanding TypeScript

TypeScript, developed by Microsoft, is a superset of JavaScript that adds static typing to the language. This enables developers to catch common errors at compile time rather than at runtime. For instance, if you try to use a string where a number is expected, TypeScript can alert you early on, potentially saving hours of debugging later.

Key Features of TypeScript:

Static Typing: Type variables to catch type errors during development.

Interfaces: Define the shape of objects and enforce type checking.

Generics: Create reusable components with type-safe flexibility.

Type Aliases: Simplify complex types for easier code readability. ## 5.2 Setting Up Your React Project with TypeScript

To get started with TypeScript in a React environment, you need to set up your development environment. The easiest way to create a new React project using TypeScript is through Create React App, which has built-in support for TypeScript.

Step 1: Create a New React App

Open your terminal and run the following command:

```bash
npx create-react-app my-app --template typescript
```

This will bootstrap a new React application with TypeScript support preconfigured. ### Step 2: Install Dependencies

If you plan to use additional libraries or frameworks, ensure you install their type definitions as well. For example, if you're using React Router, you can install its type definitions:

```bash
npm install @types/react-router-dom
```

Step 3: File Extensions

In a TypeScript React application, you will primarily work with `.tsx` files for components, as they allow the use of JSX alongside TypeScript. Regular TypeScript files will still use the `.ts` extension.

5.3 Creating Your First TypeScript Component

Let's create a simple TypeScript component to see how type definitions enhance your React code. We'll create a functional component that accepts props.

Example: Creating a Greeting Component

```tsx
import React from 'react';
interface GreetingProps { name: string;
age?: number; // Optional prop
}
const Greeting: React.FC<GreetingProps> = ({ name, age }) => { return (
<div>
<h1>Hello, {name}!</h1>
{age && <p>You are {age} years old.</p>}
</div>
);
};
export default Greeting;
```

In this example, we define a `GreetingProps` interface to specify the types of props the `Greeting` component expects. The `name` prop is required, while the `age` prop is optional. This way, if someone tries to pass invalid types as props, TypeScript will raise an error before the code is executed.

5.4 Using State and Props with TypeScript

TypeScript shines when defining and managing state and props in your components. Let's see how to work with state using the `useState` hook.

Example: Counter Component

```tsx
import React, { useState } from 'react';
const Counter: React.FC = () => {
const [count, setCount] = useState<number>(0);
const increment = () => setCount(count + 1); const decrement = () => setCount(count - 1);
return (
<div>
<h2>Count: {count}</h2>
<button onClick={increment}>Increment</button>
<button onClick={decrement}>Decrement</button>
</div>
);
};

export default Counter;
```

Here, we use the `useState` hook to manage the count state. By explicitly defining the type of the state as `number`, we ensure that only numerical values can be assigned, preventing potential bugs in our application.

5.5 Working with Context and TypeScript

React's Context API allows for global state management,

and TypeScript can help define the context's structure and type safety.

Example: Creating a Theme Context

```tsx
import React, { createContext, useContext, useState } from 'react'; type Theme = 'light' | 'dark';

interface ThemeContextType { theme: Theme;

toggleTheme: () => void;

}

const ThemeContext = createContext<ThemeContextType | undefined>(undefined); const ThemeProvider: React.FC = ({ children }) => {

const [theme, setTheme] = useState<Theme>('light');

const toggleTheme = () => {

setTheme((prev) => (prev === 'light' ? 'dark' : 'light'));

};

return (

<ThemeContext.Provider value={{ theme, toggleTheme }}>

{children}

</ThemeContext.Provider>

);

};

const useTheme = () => {

const context = useContext(ThemeContext); if (context
```

=== undefined) {

throw new Error('useTheme must be used within a ThemeProvider');

}

return context;

};

export { ThemeProvider, useTheme };

```
```

In this example, we create a `ThemeContext` with a type that defines the theme state and a function to toggle the theme. The `useTheme` hook allows components to access the context, and the TypeScript types help ensure that the context is used correctly throughout the application.

5.6 Handling Events and Form Inputs

TypeScript also enhances event handling and forms by providing type safety for event objects. ### Example: Form Component

```tsx
```

import React, { useState } from 'react';

const UserForm: React.FC = () => {

const [username, setUsername] = useState<string>('');
const [email, setEmail] = useState<string>('');

const   handleSubmit   =   (event:
React.FormEvent<HTMLFormElement>)   =>   {

```
event.preventDefault();
console.log(`Username: ${username}, Email: ${email}`);
};
return (
<form onSubmit={handleSubmit}>
<div>
<label> Username:
<input type="text"
value={username}
onChange={(e) => setUsername(e.target.value)}
/>
</label>
</div>
<div>
<label> Email:
<input type="email" value={email}
onChange={(e) => setEmail(e.target.value)}
/>
</label>
</div>
<button type="submit">Submit</button>
</form>
);
```

```
};
export default UserForm;
```
```

In this form component, we type the `event` parameter in the `handleSubmit` function as a

`React.FormEvent<HTMLFormElement>`. This informs TypeScript about the specific event being handled, allowing access to properties and methods that are safe to use with forms.

Integrating TypeScript with React can significantly enhance your development experience. By providing static typing, interfaces, and type safety, TypeScript helps you catch potential errors early, improves codereadability, and enables better collaboration among developers. In this chapter, we covered:

The benefits of using TypeScript with React.

How to set up a React project with TypeScript.

Creating components with typed props and state.

Using Context API and handling events and forms effectively.

# Setting Up TypeScript in a React Project and Using Typed Props

This chapter will guide you through the process of setting up TypeScript in a React project and illustrate how to define and use typed props effectively.

## 1. Initial Setup
```

1.1 Creating a New React Project with TypeScript

If you're starting a new React project, the easiest way to set it up with TypeScript is by using Create React App (CRA) with the TypeScript template. Open your terminal and run the following command:

```bash
npx create-react-app my-app --template typescript
```

Replace `my-app` with your desired project name. This command sets up a new React application with TypeScript configurations out of the box, including TypeScript dependencies and basic type definitions for React.

1.2 Adding TypeScript to an Existing React Project

If you have an existing React application and want to add TypeScript to it, you can do so by following these steps:

Install TypeScript and necessary types:

```bash
npm install --save typescript @types/react @types/react-dom
```

Create a `tsconfig.json` file in the root of your project. You can generate a default one with:

```bash
npx tsc --init
```

Modify your `tsconfig.json` to suit your project needs.

78

Below is a basic configuration:

```json
{
"compilerOptions": { "target": "es5",
"lib": ["dom", "dom.iterable", "esnext"], "allowJs": true,
"skipLibCheck": true, "strict": true,
"forceConsistentCasingInFileNames": true, "noEmit": true,
"esModuleInterop": true, "module": "esnext",
"moduleResolution": "node", "resolveJsonModule": true,
"isolatedModules": true, "jsx": "react-jsx"
},
"include": ["src"]
}
```

Rename your existing JSX files from `.js` or `.jsx` to `.ts` or `.tsx`, respectively.

Now, you're ready to start working with TypeScript in your React application! ## 2. Using Typed Props in React Components

One of the primary benefits of TypeScript is the ability to specify types for props in your React components, making it easier to reason about your code and catch bugs.

2.1 Defining Typed Props

Let's create a simple functional component that uses typed props.

```tsx
// src/components/Greeting.tsx import React from 'react';
// Define an interface for props interface GreetingProps {
name: string;

age: number;

}

const Greeting: React.FC<GreetingProps> = ({ name, age
}) => { return (

<div>

<h1>Hello, {name}!</h1>

<p>You are {age} years old.</p>

</div>

);

};

export default Greeting;
```

In the above code:

We define a TypeScript interface `GreetingProps` which describes the shape of the props our `Greeting` component expects.

The `Greeting` component is of type `React.FC<GreetingProps>`, which means that it will receive props defined by the `GreetingProps` interface.

2.2 Using the Component with Typed Props

Now, let's use this `Greeting` component in our main

application file.

```tsx
// src/App.tsx
import React from 'react';
import Greeting from './components/Greeting';
const App: React.FC = () => { return (
<div>
<Greeting name="Alice" age={30} ></Greeting>
<Greeting name="Bob" age={25} ></Greeting>
{/* This will cause a TypeScript error since age is not a string */}
{/* <Greeting name="Charlie" age="unknown" ></Greeting> */}
</div>
);
};
export default App;
```

In this example, if we attempt to pass an incorrect type (like a string for age), TypeScript will raise an error during development, prompting us to correct it. This ensures type safety throughout our component usage.

2.3 Default Props with TypeScript

You can also define default props in TypeScript. Here's an updated version of the `Greeting` component that includes default props:

```tsx
// src/components/Greeting.tsx import React from 'react';
interface GreetingProps { name: string;
age?: number; // Making age optional
}
const Greeting: React.FC<GreetingProps> = ({ name, age = 18 }) => { return (
<div>
<h1>Hello, {name}!</h1>
<p>You are {age} years old.</p>
</div>
);
};
export default Greeting;
```

In this version, we made `age` optional by using the `?` syntax, and we provided a default value of `18`. When `age` isn't provided, it automatically defaults to `18`.

Setting up TypeScript in a React project not only strengthens your codebase but also improves the development experience by reducing bugs and facilitating better collaboration among developers. By defining typed props for your components, you ensure that your components are used correctly and improve overall maintainability.

Managing State, Context, and Hooks with TypeScript

Adding TypeScript into the mix enhances the development experience by providing strong typing, which increases code reliability and developer productivity. This chapter will explore how to effectively manage state, context, and hooks using TypeScript in a React application.

Understanding State Management in React

React components maintain their local state using the `useState` hook, but as an application grows, managing state across components can become challenging. Local states may become cumbersome as interconnected components share the same state or if the state needs to be preserved across various parts of the application.

Local State Management

The simplest form of state management is through local state within functional components. Here's a quick refresher on using `useState` with TypeScript:

```tsx
import React, { useState } from 'react';

const Counter: React.FC = () => {

const [count, setCount] = useState<number>(0);

const increment = () => setCount(count + 1); const decrement = () => setCount(count - 1);

return (
```

```tsx
    <div>
      <h1>{count}</h1>
      <button onClick={increment}>Increment</button>
      <button onClick={decrement}>Decrement</button>
    </div>
  );
};
```

In this example, we declare a local state `count` of type `number`. TypeScript helps ensure that `setCount` can only be called with a number, enhancing type safety.

Lifting State Up

When several components need to share the same state, lifting the state to the nearest common ancestor becomes necessary. For example:

```tsx
import React, { useState } from 'react';

const Parent: React.FC = () => {
  const [count, setCount] = useState<number>(0);

  return (
    <div>
      <Child count={count} setCount={setCount} ></Child>
    </div>
```

```
);
};
interface ChildProps { count: number;
setCount:
React.Dispatch<React.SetStateAction<number>>;
}
const Child: React.FC<ChildProps> = ({ count, setCount
}) => (
<div>
<h1>{count}</h1>
<button     onClick={()     =>     setCount(count     +
1)}>Increment</button>
</div>
);
```

The `Parent` component manages the `count` state and passes it down as props to the `Child` component. This pattern encourages clear data flow, but as the app scales, passing props through multiple layers can become tedious.

Context API: Global State Management

To avoid prop-drilling (the practice of passing props down through every level of the component tree), React's Context API provides a way to pass data through the component tree without having to pass props down manually at every level. Here's how to implement the Context API with TypeScript:

Creating a Context

Create a context and provide a type for its value:

```tsx
import React, { createContext, useContext, useState, ReactNode } from 'react';

interface CounterContextType { count: number;

increment: () => void; decrement: () => void;

}

const                    CounterContext              =
createContext<CounterContextType                         |
undefined>(undefined);        const      CounterProvider:
React.FC<{ children: ReactNode }> = ({ children }) => {

const [count, setCount] = useState<number>(0);

const  increment  =  ()  =>  setCount(count + 1); const
decrement = () => setCount(count - 1);

return (

<CounterContext.Provider value={{ count, increment,
decrement }}>
{children}


</CounterContext.Provider>

);

};

const useCounter = () => {

const context = useContext(CounterContext); if (!context)
```

```tsx
{
throw new Error('useCounter must be used within a
CounterProvider');
}
return context;
};
```

Consuming the Context

Now that we have our context established, any component wrapped in `CounterProvider` can access the global counter state:

```tsx
const CounterDisplay: React.FC = () => {
const { count, increment, decrement } = useCounter();
return (
<div>
<h1>{count}</h1>
<button onClick={increment}>Increment</button>
<button onClick={decrement}>Decrement</button>
</div>
);
};
// Usage
const App: React.FC = () => (
```

```tsx
<CounterProvider>
<CounterDisplay ></CounterDisplay>
</CounterProvider>
);
```

Using Hooks for Custom Logic

While React's built-in hooks serve most purposes, creating custom hooks improves code reusability. Custom hooks provide a way to extract stateful logic from components, allowing for cleaner codebases.

Example: Custom Hook for Local Storage

Here's a custom hook that syncs state with local storage:

```tsx
import { useState, useEffect } from 'react';

function useLocalStorage<T>(key: string, initialValue: T)
{ const [storedValue, setStoredValue] = useState<T>(()
=> {


try {
const item = window.localStorage.getItem(key); return
item ? JSON.parse(item) : initialValue;
} catch (error) { return initialValue;
}
});
useEffect(() => { try {
```

```tsx
    window.localStorage.setItem(key,
JSON.stringify(storedValue));
    } catch (error) {
    console.error(`Error setting localStorage key "${key}":`,
error);
    }
  }, [key, storedValue]);
  return [storedValue, setStoredValue] as const;
}
```

Utilizing the Custom Hook

You can now use this custom hook in any component:

```tsx
const Preferences: React.FC = () => {
  const [theme, setTheme] =
useLocalStorage<string>('theme', 'light');

  return (
    <div>
      <h2>Selected Theme: {theme}</h2>
      <button onClick={() => setTheme('light')}>Light
Theme</button>
      <button onClick={() => setTheme('dark')}>Dark
Theme</button>
    </div>
  );
```

```
};
```
```
` ` `
```

We began with local state management using `useState`, explored lifting state up for shared state across components, and then transitioned into using the Context API for global state management. Finally, we touched upon creating custom hooks to encapsulate reusable stateful logic. By leveraging TypeScript, we enhance our app's reliability and maintainability, making it easier to build and scale complex frontend applications.

Chapter 6: Type-Safe Forms and Event Handling in React

With the power of React and TypeScript, developers can create not only reusable components but also maintain a high level of type safety, minimizing errors and improving code quality. In this chapter, we'll explore how to implement type-safe forms and event handling within a React application using TypeScript.

6.1 Understanding the Basics of Forms in React

To begin with, let's quickly review how forms work in React. Forms in React are typically controlled components, meaning that the form element's values are provided by the component's state. By utilizing state to control the form input values, you can easily manage user inputs and implement validation.

Here's a simple example of a controlled form in React:

```tsx
import React, { useState } from 'react';

const SimpleForm: React.FC = () => {
  const [name, setName] = useState<string>("");

  const handleChange = (event: React.ChangeEvent<HTMLInputElement>) => {
    setName(event.target.value);
  };
  const handleSubmit = (event: React.FormEvent<HTMLFormElement>) => {
```

```
event.preventDefault();
console.log('Submitted name:', name);
};
return (
<form onSubmit={handleSubmit}>
<label> Name:
<input          type="text"          value={name}
onChange={handleChange} />
</label>
<button type="submit">Submit</button>
</form>
);
};
export default SimpleForm;
```
```

In this example, we create a simple form that takes a user's name as input. The form uses local state to handle the value and updates it on each change via `handleChange`.

## 6.2 Leveraging TypeScript for Type-Safety

TypeScript provides a robust type system that can help you catch potential errors at compile-time instead of runtime. When dealing with forms, using TypeScript can help you ensure that you only accept valid types for your form inputs and handle event types appropriately.

### Defining Types for Form State
```

First, we will define a type for our form state:

```tsx
type FormState = { name: string;
};
```

Next, we can use this type in our component:

```tsx
import React, { useState } from 'react';

const TypedForm: React.FC = () => {

const [formState, setFormState] = useState<FormState>({ name: " });

const handleChange = (event: React.ChangeEvent<HTMLInputElement>) => { setFormState({ ...formState, [event.target.name]: event.target.value });
};

const handleSubmit = (event: React.FormEvent<HTMLFormElement>) => { event.preventDefault();

console.log('Submitted:', formState);
};

return (

<form onSubmit={handleSubmit}>

<label> Name:

<input type="text" name="name"
```

```tsx
value={formState.name} onChange={handleChange}
/>
</label>
<button type="submit">Submit</button>
</form>
);
};

export default TypedForm;
```

By defining the `formState` type, we ensure that any updates to the state will conform to our defined structure. If we accidentally introduce a property that does not exist in `FormState`, TypeScript will raise an error, helping us maintain the integrity of our code.

6.3 Handling Multiple Inputs

For forms with multiple inputs, it is crucial to manage the state in a more dynamic way. We can utilize computed property names in TypeScript to manage these inputs efficiently.

```tsx
import React, { useState } from 'react';

type FormState = { name: string; email: string;
};

const MultiInputForm: React.FC = () => {

const [formState, setFormState] = useState<FormState>({
name: '', email: '' });
```

```jsx
const handleChange = (event:
React.ChangeEvent<HTMLInputElement>) => { const {
name, value } = event.target;

setFormState((prevState) => ({ ...prevState, [name]: value
}));
};

const handleSubmit = (event:
React.FormEvent<HTMLFormElement>) => {
event.preventDefault();

console.log('Submitted:', formState);
};

return (

<form onSubmit={handleSubmit}>

<label> Name:

<input type="text" name="name"

value={formState.name} onChange={handleChange}

/ >

</label>

<br / >

<label> Email:

<input type="email" name="email"

value={formState.email} onChange={handleChange}

/ >

</label>

<br / >
```

```tsx
<button type="submit">Submit</button>
</form>
);
};
```

```
export default MultiInputForm;
```

In this example, we added an email input fields, demonstrating how the state can be dynamically updated based on the input name.

6.4 Validating Form Inputs

Incorporating validation into your forms is crucial for providing feedback to users. TypeScript can be utilized here as well to ensure proper validation logic.

You can create a validation function that will return an object representing the validation status for each field:

```tsx
type ValidationErrors = { name?: string;

email?: string;

};

const validateForm = (formState: FormState): ValidationErrors => { const errors: ValidationErrors = {};


if (!formState.name) { errors.name = 'Name is required';

}
```

```tsx
if (!formState.email.includes('@')) { errors.email = 'Email is invalid';
}

return errors;
};
```

You can then call this validation function in the `handleSubmit` method:

```tsx
const handleSubmit = (event: React.FormEvent<HTMLFormElement>) => {
event.preventDefault();
const errors = validateForm(formState);

if (Object.keys(errors).length > 0) {
console.log('Validation Errors:', errors); return;
}

console.log('Submitted:', formState);
};
```

By defining types for our form states and handling events, we can ensure that our code is robust and less prone to

97

errors. Adding validation enhances user experience and ensures that the data being submitted is accurate.

Handling User Input, Forms, and Validation with TypeScript

TypeScript, a superset of JavaScript, offers robust features that facilitate type safety and validation, making it an excellent choice for managing forms and user interactions. This chapter aims to walk you through the best practices for handling user input, constructing forms, and implementing validation in TypeScript.

1. Understanding Forms in TypeScript

Forms are the primary method of user interaction in web applications. They allow users to input data, which can then be processed, validated, and stored. In TypeScript, you can leverage type annotations to create well- defined interfaces that describe the structure of the data you expect from user input.

1.1 Defining a Form Model

To begin, we can define an interface that represents the structure of the form data. This provides clarity on what variables to expect.

```typescript
interface UserForm {

username: string; email: string; password: string;

agreeToTerms: boolean;

}
```

In this example, we establish a `UserForm` interface with four fields: username, email, password, and a boolean flag for agreeing to terms. Each field is typed according to the expected input.

2. Creating a Form in HTML

Creating a form in HTML is straightforward. Below is an example using basic HTML elements:

```html
<form id="userForm">
<label for="username">Username:</label>
<input type="text" id="username" name="username" required>

<label for="email">Email:</label>
<input type="email" id="email" name="email" required>

<label for="password">Password:</label>
<input type="password" id="password" name="password" required>

<label>
<input type="checkbox" id="agreeToTerms" name="agreeToTerms" required> I agree to the terms and conditions
</label>
<button type="submit">Submit</button>
```

```
</form>
```

3. Accessing Form Data

To capture user input from the form, we can add an event listener for the `submit` event and prevent the default action. Then we can gather the data and type it according to our `UserForm` interface.

```typescript
const form = document.getElementById('userForm') as HTMLFormElement;

form.addEventListener('submit', (event) => {
event.preventDefault();

const formData: UserForm = {

username: (document.getElementById('username') as HTMLInputElement).value, email: (document.getElementById('email') as HTMLInputElement).value, password: (document.getElementById('password') as HTMLInputElement).value,

agreeToTerms: (document.getElementById('agreeToTerms') as HTMLInputElement).checked,

};

console.log(formData);

});
```

In this example, we utilize type assertions to specify the

100

element types when capturing data. This ensures that TypeScript can infer the correct types for each form input.

4. Validating User Input

Validation is crucial for ensuring that the user inputs conform to the expected structure and constraints. TypeScript enables us to define validation logic that can leverage the type safety it provides.

4.1 Basic Validation Techniques

You can implement basic client-side validation by checking the properties of the `formData` object before processing it:

```typescript
function validateFormData(data: UserForm): boolean { if
(!data.username || data.username.length < 3) {

alert('Username must be at least 3 characters long.');
return false;
}


const emailPattern = /^[^\s@]+@[^\s@]+\.[^\s@]+$/;
if (!emailPattern.test(data.email)) {

alert('Please enter a valid email address.'); return false;
}


if (data.password.length < 6) {


alert('Password must be at least 6 characters long.');
```

```
    return false;

  }

  if (!data.agreeToTerms) {

    alert('You must agree to the terms and conditions.');
    return false;

  }

  return true;

}
```
```

After defining the `validateFormData` function, we can incorporate it into our form submission handling:

```typescript
form.addEventListener('submit', (event) => {

  event.preventDefault();

  const formData: UserForm = {

    username: (document.getElementById('username') as HTMLInputElement).value,
    email: (document.getElementById('email') as HTMLInputElement).value,
    password: (document.getElementById('password') as HTMLInputElement).value,

    agreeToTerms: (document.getElementById('agreeToTerms') as HTMLInputElement).checked,

  };

  if (validateFormData(formData)) {
```
```

```typescript
  console.log('Form submitted successfully!', formData);
  }
});
```

5. Advanced Validation Techniques

For more complex validation scenarios, consider using third-party libraries or custom validation functions. Libraries such as **Yup** and **Validator.js** provide hooks to integrate with your TypeScript code seamlessly.

5.1 Using Yup for Schema Validation

Here's how you can use Yup to validate form input:

```typescript
import * as Yup from 'yup';

const schema = Yup.object().shape({ username: Yup.string().min(3).required(), email: Yup.string().email().required(), password: Yup.string().min(6).required(),

agreeToTerms: Yup.boolean().oneOf([true], 'You must agree to the terms').required(),
});
// Validation implementation
form.addEventListener('submit', async (event) => {

event.preventDefault();

const formData: UserForm = {

username: (document.getElementById('username') as HTMLInputElement).value, email:
```

```
(document.getElementById('email')                    as
HTMLInputElement).value,                    password:
(document.getElementById('password')                 as
HTMLInputElement).value,

agreeToTerms:
(document.getElementById('agreeToTerms')              as
HTMLInputElement).checked,
};
try {
await schema.validate(formData);
console.log('Form submitted successfully!', formData);
} catch (error) { alert(error.errors[0]);
}
});
```
```

In this example, we define a validation schema using Yup and use it to validate the data after form submission. This encapsulates validation logic, producing clearer code and improving maintainability.

By defining interfaces, creating clear validation logic, and leveraging existing libraries, you can build robust applications that maintain data integrity. In this chapter, you've learned to create a form, gather input data, validate user inputs, and manage errors effectively. As you continue to explore TypeScript and its capabilities, these techniques will significantly enhance your web development toolkit.
```

Writing Type-Safe Event Handlers and Using React-Query

This chapter will guide you through the process of building type-safe event handlers and harnessing the power of React Query using TypeScript.

Understanding Type Safety in React

Type safety ensures that operations on data types are appropriately checked during compile-time rather than at runtime, reducing unexpected behavior in your application. TypeScript enhances JavaScript by adding a type system that helps developers catch errors early on.

When dealing with event handlers in React, type safety allows you to define the specific types of the events and their associated data. This is particularly useful when dealing with forms, user inputs, or any event- driven architecture to ensure that the data being handled adheres to expected formats.

Writing Type-Safe Event Handlers ### 1. Defining Events in TypeScript

React provides a well-defined set of synthetic events that can be typed using `React` types. Below is an example of typing a click event in a functional component.

```typescript
import React from 'react';

const MyButton: React.FC = () => {

const handleClick = (event: React.MouseEvent<HTMLButtonElement>) => {
console.log("Button clicked!", event);
```

```
};

return    <button    onClick={handleClick}>Click
Me</button>;

};
```
` ` `

2. Using Custom Event Handlers

When creating custom components, you'll often need to
define your own event handlers. By defining an interface
for your props, you can ensure type safety for props and
event-related data.

```typescript
interface MyInputProps {

onChange:                              (event:
React.ChangeEvent<HTMLInputElement>)    =>    void;
label: string;

}

const MyInput: React.FC<MyInputProps> = ({ onChange,
label }) => { return (

<label>

{label}

<input type="text" onChange={onChange} />

</label>

);

};

// Usage
```

```typescript
const Form: React.FC = () => {
  const handleInputChange = (event: React.ChangeEvent<HTMLInputElement>) => {
    console.log(event.target.value);
  };
  return <MyInput onChange={handleInputChange} label="Type something:" ></MyInput>;
};
```

3. Using Generics for Flexible Handlers

For event handlers that may work with different event types, you can employ generics. This greatly enhances reusability while still maintaining type safety.

```typescript
const handleEvent = <T extends React.SyntheticEvent<any>>(event: T) => {
  console.log(event.type);
};

const MyComponent: React.FC = () => {
  return (
    <>
      <button onClick={handleEvent}>Click Me</button>
      <input type="text" onFocus={handleEvent} />
    </>
  );
};
```

```
```

Integrating React Query with TypeScript ### 1. Setting Up React Query

React Query is a powerful library for managing server state in React applications. To use it, you first need to install it:

```bash
npm install react-query
```

2. Creating Type-Safe Queries

When using React Query, it's essential to type your data to ensure that the application adheres to a specific structure.

```typescript
import { useQuery } from 'react-query';

interface User { id: number; name: string; email: string;
}

const fetchUsers = async (): Promise<User[]> => { const response = await fetch('/api/users');

if (!response.ok) {

throw new Error('Network response was not ok');

}

return response.json();

};

const UsersList: React.FC = () => {

const { data, error, isLoading } = useQuery<User[],
```
108

```
Error>('users', fetchUsers);

if (isLoading) return <div>Loading...</div>;
if (error) return <div>Error: {error.message}</div>;
return (
<ul>
{data?.map(user => (
<li key={user.id}>
{user.name} - {user.email}
</li>
))}
</ul>
);
};
```

3. Mutations with Type Safety

When making changes to data (like creating or updating), you can use mutations. By defining types for the variables and returned data, you ensure that your updates are safe.

```typescript
import { useMutation } from 'react-query';

const addUser = async (newUser: Omit<User, 'id'>): Promise<User> => { const response = await fetch('/api/users', {
```

```
method: 'POST', headers: {
'Content-Type': 'application/json',
},
body: JSON.stringify(newUser),
});
return response.json();
};
const CreateUserForm: React.FC = () => { const mutation
= useMutation(addUser);
const handleSubmit = async (event: React.FormEvent) =>
{ event.preventDefault();
const formData = new FormData(event.target as
HTMLFormElement); const newUser = {
name: formData.get('name') as string, email:
formData.get('email') as string,
};
mutation.mutate(newUser);
};
return (
<form onSubmit={handleSubmit}>
<input name="name" placeholder="Name" required />
<input name="email" placeholder="Email" type="email"
required />
<button type="submit">Add User</button>
</form>
```

```
);
};
```
```
```

By leveraging TypeScript's type system, we ensure reliable interactions and data management, resulting in a smoother development experience and robust applications.

Chapter 7: TypeScript with Angular

Angular, a platform developed by Google, leverages TypeScript to enhance the development experience with clear benefits such as enhanced tooling, maintainability, and scalability. In this chapter, we will explore the synergy between TypeScript and Angular, detailing how to set up your environment, use TypeScript features effectively, and implement best practices for your Angular applications.

1. Setting Up Your Environment

Before diving into the use of TypeScript with Angular, you need to ensure that your development environment is correctly set up.

1.1 Installing Node.js and Angular CLI

To get started, you will need Node.js installed on your machine. The Angular CLI (Command Line Interface) is an essential tool for developing Angular applications, as it provides commands to create projects, generate components, services, and more.

Install Node.js: Download and install the latest version of Node.js from [Node.js official website](https://nodejs.org).

Install Angular CLI: Open your terminal or command prompt and execute the following command:

```bash
npm install -g @angular/cli
```

1.2 Creating a New Angular Project

With the Angular CLI installed, you can easily generate a new Angular project by running:

```bash
ng new my-angular-app
```

During the setup process, the CLI will prompt you to choose options such as routing and stylesheets (CSS, SCSS, etc.). After you make your selections, it will create a new directory with all the necessary files and configurations.

1.3 Starting the Development Server

To see your Angular application in action, navigate to your project's directory and start the development server:

```bash
cd my-angular-app ng serve
```

Once the server is running, open your browser and navigate to `http://localhost:4200`. You should see a welcome screen confirming that your Angular application is up and running.

2. Understanding TypeScript Basics

Though we will primarily focus on applying TypeScript in Angular, understanding its core concepts is crucial for effective use.

2.1 Static Typing

TypeScript introduces static typing to JavaScript, allowing you to define variable types explicitly. This helps catch errors during compile time.

Example:

```typescript
let message: string = "Hello, TypeScript!";
```

If you try to assign a different type to `message`, TypeScript will generate an error. ### 2.2 Interfaces

Interfaces are a powerful feature of TypeScript that allow you to define contracts for classes or objects. This ensures that certain properties and methods are implemented.

Example:

```typescript
interface User { id: number; name: string; email: string;
}
const user: User = { id: 1,
name: "John Doe",
email: "johndoe@example.com"
};
```

2.3 Classes and Decorators

TypeScript supports object-oriented programming with classes, which can also be complemented by Angular's decorators. Decorators allow you to add metadata to classes, methods, and properties.

Example:

```typescript
import { Component } from '@angular/core';
@Component({
selector: 'app-hello-world',
template: `<h1>Hello, World!</h1>`
})
export class HelloWorldComponent {}
```

In this example, the `@Component` decorator defines the `HelloWorldComponent` class as an Angular component, with a selector and template.

3. Building Angular Components with TypeScript

One of the foundational building blocks of an Angular application is the component. Each component encapsulates the logic and presentation of a part of your application.

3.1 Creating a Component

To create a new component using Angular CLI, execute:

```bash
ng generate component my-new-component
```

This command generates the component files and automatically registers it in the NgModule. The generated `.ts` file will look like this:

```typescript
```

```
import { Component } from '@angular/core';
@Component({
selector: 'app-my-new-component',
templateUrl:    './my-new-component.component.html',
styleUrls: ['./my-new-component.component.css']
})
export class MyNewComponent { title: string = 'My New
Component';
constructor() {}
}
```
` ` `

3.2 Component Templates and Styles

Angular components can have associated templates (HTML) and styles (CSS). Using TypeScript, you can dynamically bind data to your templates.

Example:

` ` `html

```
<h1>{{ title }}</h1>
```
` ` `

In the above example, `title` is a property defined in the component's TypeScript class. ### 3.3 Input and Output Properties

To facilitate communication between components, you can define input and output properties.

- **Input Properties**: Use the `@Input` decorator to pass data from a parent to a child component.

116

```typescript
import { Component, Input } from '@angular/core';

@Component({ selector: 'app-child',
template: `<p>{{ childMessage }}</p>`,
})
export class ChildComponent { @Input() childMessage:
string;
}
```

- **Output Properties**: Use the `@Output` decorator
and `EventEmitter` to emit events from a child to a
parent component.

```typescript
import { Component, Output, EventEmitter } from
'@angular/core';

@Component({ selector: 'app-child',

template: `<button    (click)="sendMessage()">Send
Message</button>`,
})
export class ChildComponent {

@Output() messageEvent = new EventEmitter<string>();

sendMessage() { this.messageEvent.emit('Hello Parent!');

}
}
```

```
```

4. Services and Dependency Injection

Angular's dependency injection (DI) system allows you to create services that can be shared across components. Services often provide business logic or data-fetching capabilities.

4.1 Creating a Service

Run the following command to create a service:

```bash
ng generate service my-service
```

In the generated service file, you can define methods and properties:

```typescript
import { Injectable } from '@angular/core';
@Injectable({ providedIn: 'root'
})
export class MyService { getData() {
return ['Data 1', 'Data 2', 'Data 3'];
}
}
```

4.2 Injecting a Service into a Component

To use the service in a component, inject it via the constructor:

```typescript
import { Component, OnInit } from '@angular/core';
import { MyService } from './my-service.service';
@Component({
selector: 'app-my-component',
template: `<ul><li *ngFor="let item of data">{{ item }}</li></ul>`,
})
export class MyComponent implements OnInit { data: string[];
constructor(private myService: MyService) {} ngOnInit() {
this.data = this.myService.getData();
}
}
```

5. Best Practices

Type Safety: Always define types for variables, function arguments, and return values to leverage TypeScript's static typing.

Use Interfaces: Define interfaces for complex data objects to maintain consistency across your application.

Organize Code: Structure your project with clear folder organization for components, services, models, and utilities.

Use Angular CLI: Rely on Angular CLI for code generation to follow Angular's recommended practices.

Type Annotations: Include type annotations in method parameters and return types to enhance code clarity and maintainability.

By combining the power of TypeScript with the structure of Angular, you can create scalable and maintainable web applications. As you continue your journey with Angular, embrace TypeScript's features to write cleaner, more robust code, making the most of this modern web development stack. In the next chapter, we will delve deeper into Angular routing and navigation, laying the groundwork for building more complex applications.

Integrating TypeScript in Angular Components, Services, and Modules

This chapter explores integrating TypeScript within Angular components, services, and modules, effectively utilizing type safety and modern programming paradigms.

1. Setting Up an Angular Project with TypeScript

Before diving into specific Angular constructs, it's essential to set up an Angular project that uses TypeScript.

1.1 Installing Angular CLI

The Angular Command Line Interface (CLI) is a powerful tool that simplifies project setup and development. To create a new Angular project, ensure you have Node.js installed, then run:

```bash
npm install -g @angular/cli ng new my-angular-app

cd my-angular-app
```

```
```

The Angular CLI insists on using TypeScript by default, setting up an ideal starting point for your Angular application.

1.2 Project Structure Overview

On creating your Angular project, take a moment to examine the generated structure:

src/app: Contains all your components, services, and modules.

src/environments: Holds environment-specific configurations.

tsconfig.json: The TypeScript configuration file that determines how TypeScript compiles your code. Understanding this structure helps manage your resources effectively.

2. Working with Components

Angular components are the building blocks of an Angular application. Each component consists of an HTML template, a CSS style sheet, and a TypeScript class.

2.1 Creating a Component

Using Angular CLI, you can easily generate a new component:

```bash
ng generate component my-component
```

This command creates a new directory for your component inside the `src/app` folder, complete with the necessary files.

2.2 Defining a Component Class with TypeScript

The generated component class (`my-component.component.ts`) will look like this:

```typescript
import { Component } from '@angular/core';

@Component({
selector: 'app-my-component',
templateUrl: './my-component.component.html',
styleUrls: ['./my-component.component.css']
})
export class MyComponent {
title: string = 'Hello, Angular with TypeScript!';
}
```

Key Elements:

The `title` property is explicitly typed as a string.

Using decorators like `@Component` allows you to define the metadata for the component. ### 2.3 Utilizing Interfaces and Types

TypeScript's ability to define types is one of its most powerful features. Here's how to use interfaces within components:

```typescript
interface User { name: string; age: number;
}
```

```
export class MyComponent { user: User = {
name: 'John', age: 30
};
}
```
```

This ensures that the `user` object adheres to the `User` interface, adding a layer of type safety. ## 3. Creating Services

Services in Angular are used to encapsulate business logic and share data between components. Integrating TypeScript here enhances maintainability.

### 3.1 Generating a Service

The Angular CLI can generate a service for you:

```bash
ng generate service my-service
```

This command creates `my-service.service.ts`, ready for implementation. ### 3.2 Defining a Service Class with TypeScript

Within your service file, you can utilize TypeScript to define and implement service logic.

```typescript
import { Injectable } from '@angular/core';
@Injectable({ providedIn: 'root'
})
```
```

```typescript
export class MyService { private data: string[] = [];
addData(newData:        string):        void       {
this.data.push(newData);
}
getData(): string[] { return this.data;
}
}
```

3.3 Using Dependency Injection

Angular's dependency injection (DI) system works seamlessly with TypeScript. You can use our service in a component:

```typescript
import { Component } from '@angular/core'; import { MyService } from './my-service.service';

@Component({
selector: 'app-my-component',
templateUrl: './my-component.component.html'
})
export class MyComponent { constructor(private myService: MyService) {}
addItem(item: string) { this.myService.addData(item);
}
}
```

Here, TypeScript automatically detects that `myService` is of the type `MyService`, enabling proper IntelliSense and type checks in the editor.

4. Structuring Modules

Modules in Angular help organize the application, encapsulating related components, directives, and services.

4.1 Creating a Module

You can create a new module using:

```bash
ng generate module my-module
```

4.2 Defining a TypeScript module

A module in Angular defines its components and services. Here's how you could define a simple module with TypeScript:

```typescript
import { NgModule } from '@angular/core';
import { CommonModule } from '@angular/common';
import { MyComponent } from './my-component/my-component.component';

@NgModule({
declarations: [MyComponent], imports: [CommonModule], exports: [MyComponent]
})
export class MyModule {}
```

```
```

The `@NgModule()` decorator specifies metadata about the module, such as declared components and imported modules.

5. Making the Most of TypeScript Features ### 5.1 Generics

TypeScript generics provide a way to create components and services that can work with any data type. By incorporating generics, you can improve the reusability of your code.

5.2 Advanced Types

Use TypeScript's advanced types like union types, intersection types, and type guards to enforce stricter types and improve code reliability.

5.3 Enums

Define enumerated types in your code for better clarity and maintenance.

```typescript
typescript enum UserRole{ Admin,

User, Guest
}


// Usage:

const currentRole: UserRole = UserRole.Admin;
```
```

Integrating TypeScript in Angular components, services, and modules significantly enhances your development
```

experience. You gain the benefits of type safety, error-checking at compile time, and improved code organization.

Enforcing Type Safety in Dependency Injection and Observables

TypeScript provides robust tools that can help enforce type safety in these areas, leading to more predictable and maintainable code. This chapter delves into how to effectively leverage TypeScript's features to ensure type safety in both Dependency Injection and Observables.

Understanding Dependency Injection

Dependency Injection is a design pattern that allows a class to receive its dependencies from an external source rather than creating them itself. In TypeScript, this pattern can be enhanced through interfaces and classes, enabling compile-time checking of the types involved in the injection process.

Defining Interfaces for Dependencies

To enforce type safety in DI, we start by defining interfaces for our services. This serves as a contract that any implementing class must fulfill.

```typescript
// Defining an interface for a service interface
LoggerService {

log(message: string): void;

}
```

```
class ConsoleLogger implements LoggerService {
log(message: string): void {

console.log(message);

}

}
```
` ` `

Implementing Dependency Injection

With the interface in place, we can utilize DI to inject the dependency into a class that requires it. TypeScript ensures that the injected service conforms to the expected type.

```typescript
class UserService {

constructor(private logger: LoggerService) {}

createUser(username: string): void { this.logger.log(`User ${username} created.`);

}

}
// Injecting dependency

const logger: LoggerService = new ConsoleLogger(); const userService = new UserService(logger); userService.createUser('Alice');
```
` ` `

In the above example, if we attempted to inject a service that did not implement `LoggerService`, TypeScript would throw an error at compile-time, helping to catch

128

potential issues early in the development cycle.

Using Decorators with DI

In frameworks like Angular, decorators can be used to simplify the DI process. TypeScript's metadata reflection capabilities allow you to declare types directly in the constructor parameters using the

`@Injectable` decorator.

```typescript
import { Injectable } from '@angular/core';
@Injectable({ providedIn: 'root',
})
class UserService {
constructor(private logger: LoggerService) {}
createUser(username: string): void { this.logger.log(`User ${username} created.`);
}
}
```

By annotating your services with `@Injectable`, you ensure that Angular's DI system respects the type and integrity of the dependency, and you benefit from full type checking at compile time.

Observables and Type Safety

Observables are a fundamental part of reactive programming, allowing asynchronous data streams and event handling. In TypeScript, you can leverage strong typing with Observables to ensure that the data being emitted adheres to a defined structure.

Creating Typed Observables

When defining an observable, you can specify the type of data it will emit. This is crucial for ensuring that consumers of the observable are aware of the data shape they will receive.

```typescript
import { Observable, of } from 'rxjs';

// Define a type interface User { id: number;

username: string;

}

// Create a typed observable

const users$: Observable<User[]> = of([{ id: 1, username: 'Alice' }, { id: 2, username: 'Bob' }]);

users$.subscribe(users => { users.forEach(user => {

console.log(`User ID: ${user.id}, Username: ${user.username}`);

});

});
```

In this example, we create an observable that emits an array of `User` objects. If an attempt is made to emit a value of a different type, TypeScript will enforce the type constraints, minimizing runtime errors.

Handling Observables with Type Safety

130

When dealing with observables, operators such as `map`, `filter`, and `flatMap` can also benefit from type safety. Type assertion ensures that transformations remain type-checked.

```typescript
import { map } from 'rxjs/operators';

// Transforming an Observable

const usernames$: Observable<string[]> = users$.pipe(
map(users => users.map(user => user.username))
);

usernames$.subscribe(usernames                =>                {
usernames.forEach(username => {

console.log(`Username: ${username}`);

});

});
```

Comprehensive Type Safety with Generics

Using generics in observables allows even greater flexibility and type accuracy, especially when creating reusable services.

```typescript
class ApiService<T> {

constructor(private httpClient: HttpClient) {}

getData(url:    string):    Observable<T>    {    return
this.httpClient.get<T>(url);

}
```

```
}
// Usage with specific types
const          userApiService          =          new
ApiService<User>(httpClient);
userApiService.getData('/api/users').subscribe(users => {
users.forEach(user => { console.log(user.username);
});
});
` ` `
```

By adhering to these principles, teams can improve their development workflows, reduce bugs, and increase confidence in their codebases, leading to a more efficient and enjoyable development experience.

Chapter 8: TypeScript with Vue.js

In this chapter, we will explore how to integrate TypeScript with Vue.js, outline the benefits of using TypeScript in your Vue projects, and provide practical examples to help you get started.

Why Use TypeScript with Vue.js?

Vue.js is known for its simplicity and flexibility, making it an excellent choice for building interactive user interfaces. However, as applications grow larger and more complex, the dynamic nature of JavaScript can lead to bugs that are often discovered only during runtime. This is where TypeScript shines, providing static typing and advanced features that can catch errors at compile time, improving overall code quality and maintainability.

Benefits of Using TypeScript with Vue.js

Type Safety: TypeScript catches type-related errors during development, reducing runtime errors and bugs in production.

Enhanced IDE Support: Integrated Development Environments (IDEs) can provide better autocompletion, refactoring capabilities, and inline documentation when using TypeScript.

Improved Documentation: Type annotations serve as self-documenting code, making it easier for developers to understand the expected types of variables, function arguments, and return values.

Scalability: As projects grow, the structured nature of TypeScript helps maintain code clarity and organization,

133

making it easier to scale applications.

Future-Proofing: TypeScript supports many modern JavaScript features, making it easier for developers to write future-proof code.

Setting Up a Vue.js Project with TypeScript

To get started, we'll set up a new Vue.js project that includes TypeScript support using Vue CLI. Follow these steps:

Step 1: Install Vue CLI

If you haven't installed Vue CLI yet, you can do so using npm:

```bash
npm install -g @vue/cli
```

Step 2: Create a New Vue Project with TypeScript

Now, create a new Vue project and configure TypeScript during the setup process:

```bash
vue create my-typescript-vue-app
```

During the prompts, select "Manually select features" and choose TypeScript along with any other features you require (e.g., Vue Router, Vuex, etc.).

Step 3: Navigate to the Project Directory

After the project is created, navigate to the project folder:

```bash
```

```bash
cd my-typescript-vue-app
```

Step 4: Start the Development Server

Start the local development server to see your Vue application in action:

```bash
npm run serve
```

You should now see a default Vue application running in your browser. ## Building a Simple Component with TypeScript

Now that we have our Vue project set up with TypeScript, let's create a simple Vue component to demonstrate how to use TypeScript effectively.

Step 1: Create a New Component

Create a new file called `HelloWorld.vue` inside the `src/components` directory. This file will contain our component code.

```html
<template>
<div>
<h1>{{ greeting }}</h1>
<button                 @click="changeGreeting">Change Greeting</button>
</div>
</template>
```

```
<script lang="ts">
import { defineComponent } from 'vue';
export default defineComponent({ name: 'HelloWorld',
data() { return {
greeting: 'Hello, Vue with TypeScript!'
};
},
methods: { changeGreeting() {
this.greeting = 'You changed the greeting!';
}
}
});
</script>
<style scoped> h1 {
color: #42b983;
}
</style>
```

Step 2: Use the Component

Next, include the `HelloWorld` component in your `App.vue` file:

```html
<template>
```

```
<div id="app">
<HelloWorld ></HelloWorld>
</div>
</template>
<script lang="ts">
import { defineComponent } from 'vue';
import HelloWorld from './components/HelloWorld.vue';
export default defineComponent({ name: 'App',
components: { HelloWorld
}
});
</script>
<style> #app {
font-family: Avenir, Helvetica, Arial, sans-serif; text-align:
center;
color: #2c3e50; margin-top: 60px;
}
</style>
```
```

## TypeScript in Vue 3: Composition API

With Vue 3, the Composition API was introduced, offering a new way to compose logic in components. TypeScript pairs beautifully with the Composition API, allowing for a more organized and type-safe approach to component development. Here's an example using the Composition
```

API.

Example: Using the Composition API with TypeScript

We'll refactor the `HelloWorld` component using the Composition API.

```html
<template>
<div>
<h1>{{ greeting }}</h1>
<button @click="changeGreeting">Change Greeting</button>
</div>
</template>
<script lang="ts">
import { defineComponent, ref } from 'vue';
export default defineComponent({ name: 'HelloWorld',
setup() {
const greeting = ref<string>('Hello, Vue with TypeScript!');
const changeGreeting = () => {
greeting.value = 'You changed the greeting!';
};
return { greeting, changeGreeting
};
```

```
}
});
</script>
<style scoped> h1 {
color: #42b983;
}
</style>
` ` `
```

In this version of the component, we use the `ref` function to create a reactive `greeting` variable. The function `setup` is the entry point for using the Composition API, encapsulating the component's logic.

Integrating TypeScript with Vue.js offers a range of benefits that enhance the development experience and improve code quality. With features like type safety, better tooling, and improved code organization, TypeScript can significantly elevate your Vue projects.

Setting Up TypeScript in Vue 3 and Using the Composition API

This chapter will guide you through the process of setting up TypeScript in a Vue 3 project and utilizing the Composition API to create a scalable and maintainable application. We'll cover everything from initial setup to creating reactive components with TypeScript's strong typing and composable features.

1. Setting Up Your Vue 3 Project with TypeScript

1.1 Installing Vue CLI

To get started, we will use the Vue CLI, which simplifies project initialization. If you haven't installed it yet, you can do so using npm or yarn:

```bash
npm install -g @vue/cli # or
yarn global add @vue/cli
```

1.2 Creating a New Project

Create a new Vue 3 project with TypeScript using the command line:

```bash
vue create my-vue-ts-app
```

During the setup process, you will be prompted to select features for your new project. Choose TypeScript, and you can also select the Composition API if it is available in the options.

```text
? Please pick a preset:
Default ([Vue 2] babel, eslint)
Default (Vue 3) ([Vue 3] babel, eslint) Manually select features
```

If you choose to manually select features, ensure you

check the "TypeScript" and "Router" options if your application will use routing.

1.3 Navigating into Your Project

Once the project is created successfully, navigate into your project directory:

```bash
cd my-vue-ts-app
```

1.4 Running the Development Server

You can now run your development server to see your Vue application in action:

```bash
npm run serve # or

yarn serve
```

Open your browser and navigate to `http://localhost:8080` (or the port specified in your terminal) to see your Vue app running.

2. Exploring TypeScript in Vue 3 ### 2.1 TypeScript Configuration

After setting up your project, you should find a `tsconfig.json` file in the root of your project that contains default TypeScript configuration. Feel free to customize it based on the needs of your application.

2.2 Using TypeScript in Vue Components

In Vue 3, you can use TypeScript both in the Options API

and the Composition API. The Composition API is a more flexible and feature-rich approach to define component logic.

3. Implementing the Composition API ### 3.1 Understanding the Composition API

The Composition API allows developers to create reusable logic and maintain cleaner code. It introduces

functions such as `reactive`, `ref`, `computed`, and `watch`, which provide enhanced reactivity.

3.2 Creating a Simple Component

Create a new file called `HelloWorld.vue` in the `src/components` directory. This file will be a simple component demonstrating the Composition API with TypeScript.

```vue
<template>
<div>
<h1>{{ message }}</h1>
<input v-model="message" placeholder="Edit me!" />
</div>
</template>
<script lang="ts">
import { defineComponent, ref } from 'vue';
export default defineComponent({ setup() {
const message = ref<string>('Hello, Vue 3 with TypeScript!');
```

```
return { message
};
}
});
</script>
<style scoped> h1 {
color: #42b983;
}
</style>
` ` `
```

3.3 Explanation of the Component Code

Template: The template section contains a simple heading and an input. The input binds dynamically to the `message` variable, showcasing two-way data binding.

Script:

The component imports `defineComponent` and `ref` from Vue.

The `setup` function is where you define your reactive properties and computed values. We define

`message` as a reactive reference of type `string` using `ref`.

Finally, the `setup` function returns an object containing the properties and methods to expose to the template.

3.4 Using the Component

To use this `HelloWorld` component, import it into your `App.vue`:

```vue
<template>
<div id="app">
<HelloWorld ></HelloWorld>
</div>
</template>
<script lang="ts">
import { defineComponent } from 'vue';
import HelloWorld from './components/HelloWorld.vue';
export default defineComponent({ components: {
HelloWorld
}
});
</script>
```

4. Benefits of Using TypeScript with Vue 3 ### 4.1 Strong Typing

TypeScript provides static types that enable you to catch errors early in the development process. This minimizes runtime errors and enhances code quality.

4.2 Improved IDE Support

With TypeScript, you gain better autocompletion, inline documentation, and refactoring capabilities, making your

144

development experience more productive.

4.3 Scalability

The Composition API provides a more flexible way to build components, enabling better organization of logic and easier reuse of code across different components.

The Composition API enhances your ability to manage component logic effectively. In this chapter, we explored the fundamentals of setting up a Vue 3 project with TypeScript and demonstrated how to use the Composition API to create a simple yet functional component.

Creating Strongly Typed Vuex/Pinia Store and Components

In this chapter, we will explore how to create a strongly typed store using both Vuex and Pinia, as well as how to connect this store with TypeScript-based components, ensuring type safety and better developer experience.

Understanding TypeScript

TypeScript is a strict syntactical superset of JavaScript that adds static typing to the language. By using TypeScript in your Vue.js applications, you gain the advantages of type checking during development, which can help catch errors early in the development process, improve code readability, and enhance the collaboration experience between developers.

Why Use Strong Typing with Vuex/Pinia?

Error Detection: TypeScript helps catch errors at

compile time rather than runtime.

Better Autocompletion: IDEs can provide better autocompletion suggestions when working with typed objects.

Enhanced Documentation: Types act as a form of documentation, making the code easier to understand for new developers.

Maintainability: As your application grows, type safety aids in maintaining the codebase by providing clear contracts.

Setting Up TypeScript with Vuex ### 1. Install Dependencies

To create a strongly typed Vuex store, start by ensuring you have Vue, Vuex, and TypeScript installed in your project:

```bash
npm install vue@next vuex@next typescript --save
```

2. Define Types

Define the types for the state, mutations, actions, and getters of your Vuex store. This helps clarify what data is stored and the shape it should take.

```typescript
// store/types.ts

export interface State { count: number;

}
```

```typescript
export enum MutationTypes { INCREMENT = "INCREMENT", DECREMENT = "DECREMENT",

}
export type Mutations<S = State> = {
[MutationTypes.INCREMENT](state: S): void;
[MutationTypes.DECREMENT](state: S): void;
};
export type Actions = {
increment(context: { commit: Commit }): void;
decrement(context: { commit: Commit }): void;
};
```

3. Create the Store

Now, create the Vuex store using the types defined above.

```typescript
// store/index.ts
import { createStore } from 'vuex';
import { State, Mutations, MutationTypes } from './types';
const state: State = { count: 0,
};
const mutations: Mutations<State> = {
[MutationTypes.INCREMENT](state) { state.count++;
},
[MutationTypes.DECREMENT](state) { state.count--;
```

147

```
  },
};
const store = createStore({ state,
mutations,
});
export default store;
```

4. Use the Store in Components

To use the Vuex store in a component, you can leverage TypeScript's capabilities to ensure strong typing.

```typescript
// components/Counter.vue
<template>
<div>
<p>Count: {{ count }}</p>
<button @click="increment">Increment</button>
<button @click="decrement">Decrement</button>
</div>
</template>
<script lang="ts">
import { defineComponent } from 'vue'; import { useStore } from 'vuex';
import { State, MutationTypes } from '../store/types';
export default defineComponent({ setup() {
```

```
const store = useStore<State>();

const increment = () => {
store.commit(MutationTypes.INCREMENT);
};
const decrement = () => {
store.commit(MutationTypes.DECREMENT);
};
return {
count: store.state.count, increment,
decrement,
};
},
});
</script>
```
` ` `

Setting Up TypeScript with Pinia

Pinia has a simpler API and is designed to work seamlessly with TypeScript. Below, we will explore how to set up a strongly typed store using Pinia.

1. Install Dependencies

Ensure you have Pinia and TypeScript installed:

` ` `bash
npm install pinia --save

```
```

2. Define the Store

You can define a store in Pinia with strong typing using the `defineStore` function.

```typescript
// store/counter.ts

import { defineStore } from 'pinia';

export const useCounterStore = defineStore('counter', {
state: () => ({

count: 0,

}),

actions: { increment() { this.count++;

},

decrement() { this.count--;

},

},

});
```

3. Use the Store in Components

Integrating the Pinia store in components is similarly straightforward.

```typescript
// components/Counter.vue

<template>
```

```
<div>
<p>Count: {{ count }}</p>
<button @click="increment">Increment</button>
<button @click="decrement">Decrement</button>
</div>
</template>
<script lang="ts">
import { defineComponent } from 'vue';
import { useCounterStore } from '../store/counter';
export default defineComponent({ setup() {
const counter = useCounterStore();
return {
count: counter.count, increment: counter.increment, decrement: counter.decrement,
};
},
});
</script>
```

By providing strong type definitions for state, actions, and mutations, developers can write safer and more predictable code. In this chapter, we've explored how to establish a strongly typed store with both Vuex and Pinia and how to connect this store with typed components.

Chapter 9: Ensuring Type-Safe API Interactions

In this chapter, we will explore how to ensure type-safe API interactions in front-end applications using TypeScript.

9.1 Understanding Type Safety

Type safety refers to the extent to which a programming language discourages or prevents type errors—mistakes that occur when values are of an unexpected type. In JavaScript, due to its dynamic typing, this can lead to several runtime errors that are often only caught during execution. TypeScript introduces static typing, allowing developers to define the types of variables, function parameters, and return values at compile time.

By leveraging TypeScript in our front-end applications, we can:

Catch type-related errors during development.

Improve code readability by providing clear type definitions.

Enhance IDE features like autocompletion and inline documentation. ## 9.2 Setting Up Type Definitions for APIs

APIs usually provide structured data, and to ensure type-safe interactions, we need to define types that reflect the structure of the data we expect. This involves creating interfaces or type aliases for the different API responses we expect from our backend.

9.2.1 Defining Interfaces

Let's say we are working with a RESTful API that provides user information. We can define a TypeScript interface to represent the user data:

```typescript
interface User {
```

id: number; name: string; email: string; createdAt: Date;

}

```
```

9.2.2 Using Type Definitions with Fetch

When we fetch data from an API, we can ensure that the response conforms to our defined type. Here's how to perform a type-safe fetch operation:

```typescript
```

async function fetchUser(userId: number): Promise<User> {

const response = await fetch(`https://api.example.com/users/${userId}`);

if (!response.ok) {

throw new Error('Network response was not ok');

}

const user: User = await response.json(); return user;

}

```
```

In this example, TypeScript ensures that the `fetchUser` function always returns a `User` object. If the response does not conform to the `User` interface, TypeScript will

153

raise a compile-time error.

9.3 Handling API Errors Gracefully

In addition to ensuring types with successful API responses, it's also vital to handle errors gracefully. We can define a custom error type that represents potential API errors:

9.3.1 Defining API Error Types

```typescript
interface ApiError {

message: string; status: number;

}

async function fetchUser(userId: number): Promise<User | ApiError> { const response = await fetch(`https://api.example.com/users/${userId}`);

if (!response.ok) {

const error: ApiError = {

message: 'Failed to fetch user data', status: response.status,

};

return error;

}

const user: User = await response.json(); return user;

}
```

In this example, we modify the return type of the `fetchUser` function to indicate that it can return either a

`User` object or an `ApiError`. This way, the caller can handle both successful responses and errors in a type-safe manner.

9.4 Implementing a Generic API Handler

To reduce redundancy and streamline our API requests, we can implement a generic API handler. This generic function can handle various API calls, ensuring that they return the correct type based on the provided endpoint and response type.

9.4.1 Creating a Generic API Function

```typescript
async function apiFetch<T>(url: string): Promise<T | ApiError> { const response = await fetch(url);

if (!response.ok) { return {

message: 'Network error occurred', status: response.status,

} as ApiError;
}
return (await response.json()) as T;
}
```

9.4.2 Using the Generic API Function

Now, we can use our `apiFetch` function to fetch different types of data, ensuring type safety across our application:

```typescript
async function getUser(userId: number): Promise<User |
```

```typescript
ApiError> {                                    return
apiFetch<User>(`https://api.example.com/users/${userI
d}`);
}

async function getAllUsers(): Promise<User[] | ApiError>
{                                              return
apiFetch<User[]>(`https://api.example.com/users`);
}
```

In these examples, the API function will automatically infer the correct return type based on the generic type parameter provided.

9.5 Integrating with a State Management Solution

When dealing with API interactions in a front-end application, especially in larger applications, it's common to integrate with a state management solution such as Redux or Zustand. Here, we can ensure type-safe interactions with API responses throughout our state management logic.

9.5.1 Defining State Types

We can define the state shape of our application concerning the user data:

```typescript
interface AppState {
users: User[]; loading: boolean; error: ApiError | null;
}
```

9.5.2 Dispatching Actions with Type Safety

When dispatching actions to update the state based on API interactions, we can ensure that only valid types are passed:

```typescript
type Action =
| { type: 'FETCH_USERS_REQUEST' }
| { type: 'FETCH_USERS_SUCCESS'; payload: User[] }
| { type: 'FETCH_USERS_FAILURE'; payload: ApiError };

function reducer(state: AppState, action: Action): AppState { switch (action.type) {
case 'FETCH_USERS_REQUEST':

return { ...state, loading: true }; case 'FETCH_USERS_SUCCESS':

return { ...state, loading: false, users: action.payload }; case 'FETCH_USERS_FAILURE':

return { ...state, loading: false, error: action.payload }; default:

return state;

}

}
```

With this structure, TypeScript ensures that no invalid actions can be dispatched, effectively enhancing the reliability of our state management.

By defining types and interfaces for API responses and implementing generic functions, developers can

157

significantly reduce runtime errors and improve their development experience. Moreover, integrating these type-safe patterns with state management solutions creates a solid foundation for building scalable applications.

Defining API Response Types and Handling Asynchronous Calls

TypeScript, with its static typing system, provides a powerful way to define API response types and manage asynchronous calls effectively. This chapter will explore how to define types for API responses, leverage TypeScript features for better code quality, and manage asynchronous requests seamlessly.

Understanding Asynchronous Programming in TypeScript

Asynchronous programming allows for non-blocking calls, which is crucial when handling network requests. In JavaScript and TypeScript, there are several ways to handle asynchronous calls, most notably with

`Promises` and `async/await`. ### Promises

A `Promise` is an object representing the eventual completion (or failure) of an asynchronous operation. Here's a simple example:

```typescript
function fetchData(url: string): Promise<Response> {
return fetch(url);
}
```

```typescript
fetchData('https://api.example.com/data')
.then(response => { if (!response.ok) {
throw new Error('Network response was not ok');
}
return response.json();
})
.then(data => console.log(data))
.catch(error => console.error('There was a problem with
the fetch operation:', error));
```

Async/Await

The `async`/`await` syntax offers a more readable way to work with asynchronous code. Functions declared with `async` return a `Promise`, and within these functions, `await` can be used to pause execution until a Promise is resolved.

Here's the same example using `async/await`:

```typescript
async function fetchData(url: string): Promise<any> {
const response = await fetch(url);
if (!response.ok) {
throw new Error('Network response was not ok');
}
return await response.json();
}
```

```
async function getData() { try {
const          data          =          await
fetchData('https://api.example.com/data');
console.log(data);
} catch (error) {
console.error('There was a problem with the fetch
operation:', error);
}
}
getData();
```

Defining API Response Types

One of the key benefits of TypeScript is the ability to define types for data structures. When working with APIs, it's essential to define response types to improve the reliability of your code.

Step 1: Analyzing API Responses

Before defining types, it's critical to understand the structure of the API responses. For instance, consider an API that returns user data as follows:

```json
{
"id": 1,
"name": "John Doe",
"email": "john@example.com", "isActive": true
}
```

```
```

Step 2: Creating Type Definitions

You can create TypeScript interfaces to represent the structure of the data returned by the API. Here's how you could define a `User` type based on the JSON structure:

```typescript
interface User {

id: number; name: string; email: string; isActive: boolean;

}
```

Step 3: Using Type Definitions

Now that you have defined the `User` type, you can incorporate it into your API call function. This provides both type safety and code clarity.

```typescript
async function fetchUser(userId: number): Promise<User> {

const response = await fetch(`https://api.example.com/users/${userId}`); if (!response.ok) {

throw new Error('Network response was not ok');

}

return await response.json() as User;

}

// Usage

async function displayUser(userId: number) { try {
```

161

```
const user = await fetchUser(userId);

console.log(`User    Name:    ${user.name},    Email:
${user.email}`);

} catch (error) { console.error(error);

}

}

displayUser(1);
```
```

## Handling API Errors

Error handling is a vital aspect of API calls. You should consider both network errors and unexpected response formats.

### Step 1: Enhanced Error Handling

You can improve error handling by creating a custom error type that can convey more information about the error that occurred:

```typescript
class ApiError extends Error {

constructor(public message: string, public statusCode?:
number) { super(message);

this.name = 'ApiError';

}

}

async function fetchUserWithErrorHandling(userId:
number): Promise<User> { const response = await
fetch(`https://api.example.com/users/${userId}`);
```
```

```typescript
if (!response.ok) {
  throw new ApiError('Network response was not ok', response.status);
}
const data: User = await response.json(); return data;
}
```

Step 2: Catching Errors

When you invoke the API call, you should handle any potential errors gracefully:

```typescript
async function displayUserWithErrorHandling(userId: number) {

  try {
    const user = await fetchUserWithErrorHandling(userId);
    console.log(`User Name: ${user.name}, Email: ${user.email}`);
  } catch (error) {
    if (error instanceof ApiError) {
      console.error(`API Error: ${error.message}, Status Code: ${error.statusCode}`);
    } else {
      console.error('Unexpected Error:', error);
```

```
}
  }
}
displayUserWithErrorHandling(2);
```
```

We took advantage of TypeScript's type definitions to enhance code quality, predictability, and maintainability. As you build applications that interact with APIs, applying these principles will lead to a much more robust and error-resistant codebase.

By mastering these concepts, you'll be well-equipped to handle complex API integrations in TypeScript and create seamless user experiences in your applications.

# Fetching Data Securely with Fetch, Axios, and GraphQL in TypeScript

In this chapter, we will explore three popular methods for data fetching: the Fetch API, Axios, and GraphQL. We will implement these methods using TypeScript, enhancing our code with static type-checking, which can catch many errors at compile time rather than runtime.

## 1. Understanding the Basics of Data Fetching

Before diving into the different methods, it's important to understand some of the fundamental concepts of data fetching. Data fetching usually involves making HTTP requests to a server and retrieving data formatted as JSON. Each method we discuss here will conform to this principle but differ in syntax, features, and ease of use.
```

Security Concerns

When fetching data, security should always be a priority. Common threats include:

Cross-Site Scripting (XSS): Ensure your application properly sanitizes data from external sources.

Cross-Site Request Forgery (CSRF): Implement protective measures, such as tokens or same-site cookies, to prevent unauthorized actions.

Sensitive Data Exposure: Avoid exposing sensitive information in your requests or responses. ## 2. Fetch API

Introduction to Fetch

The Fetch API is a native browser interface for making HTTP requests. It is simple to use and supports modern features like promises and async/await syntax.

Fetching Data with TypeScript

To start using the Fetch API in a TypeScript application, you first need to install TypeScript if you haven't already. You can then create a function to fetch data:

```typescript
async function fetchData(url: string): Promise<any> { try {

const response = await fetch(url, { method: 'GET',

headers: {

'Content-Type': 'application/json',

'Authorization': `Bearer YOUR_API_TOKEN` // Example of securing API with a token
```

```
    },
  });
  if (!response.ok) {
    throw new Error(`HTTP error! Status: ${response.status}`);
  }
  const data = await response.json(); return data;
  } catch (error) {
  console.error('Fetch error:', error);
  throw error; // Rethrow for further handling
  }
}
```

Key Points

Use the `Authorization` header to send tokens securely.

Always handle response statuses to deal with errors properly. ## 3. Axios

Introduction to Axios

Axios is a popular JavaScript library for making HTTP requests. It is promise-based and includes features such as interceptors and simplified error handling, making it a robust choice for large-scale applications.

Using Axios in TypeScript

You can install Axios using npm or yarn:

```bash
```

npm install axios
```

Here's how to fetch data using Axios:
```typescript
import axios, { AxiosResponse } from 'axios';

async function fetchAxioData(url: string): Promise<any> {
try {
const response: AxiosResponse<any> = await axios.get(url, { headers: {
'Content-Type': 'application/json', 'Authorization': `Bearer YOUR_API_TOKEN`
}
});
return response.data; // Axios automatically parses JSON
} catch (error: any) { console.error('Axios error:', error);
throw error; // Rethrow for further handling
}
}
```

Key Advantages

Axios automatically transforms response data, meaning you don't need to call `.json()`.

Interceptors can be used for adding logic before requests or after responses globally.

4. GraphQL
```

Introduction to GraphQL

GraphQL is a query language for APIs that allows clients to request exactly the data they need. It is often used in combination with libraries like Apollo Client in TypeScript projects.

Setting Up Apollo Client

To get started, you need to install Apollo Client:

```bash
npm install @apollo/client graphql
```

You can create a client and define your queries like this:

```typescript
import { ApolloClient, InMemoryCache, gql } from '@apollo/client';
const client = new ApolloClient({
uri: 'YOUR_GRAPHQL_ENDPOINT',
cache: new InMemoryCache(), headers: {
'Authorization': `Bearer YOUR_API_TOKEN`
}
});
const GET_DATA = gql` query GetData {
data { id title
content
}
```

```
}
`;
async function fetchGraphQLData() { try {
const response = await client.query({ query: GET_DATA,
});
return response.data;
} catch (error) {
console.error('GraphQL error:', error); throw error; //
Rethrow for further handling
}
}
```

Benefits of Using GraphQL

Clients can specify exactly which data they need, reducing over-fetching.

Strongly typed schema enhances error checking and removes ambiguity in data structures. ## 5. Best Practices for Secure Data Fetching

Use HTTPS

Always use HTTPS to encrypt data in transit. This protects against man-in-the-middle attacks. ### Handle Errors Gracefully

Regardless of the method you use, proper error handling is crucial. Use try-catch blocks, and consider user-friendly messages to inform the user of issues without exposing sensitive error details.

Validate and Sanitize Data

Always validate and sanitize any data received from external APIs. This prevents XSS and other injection attacks.

Token Management

If using tokens for authentication, store them securely (e.g., in memory or secure storage). Avoid exposing them publicly, and consider using refresh tokens.

By incorporating secure data fetching practices, we ensure our applications remain robust and reliable. In the next chapter, we will delve into error handling strategies to create more resilient applications.

Chapter 10: Scalable Architecture with TypeScript

The rise of JavaScript as a dominant language for web development has been significant, but with the increasing complexity of applications, coupling JavaScript's dynamic nature with TypeScript's static typing presents developers with a robust and scalable framework.

10.1 Introduction to TypeScript

TypeScript, developed by Microsoft, is a superset of JavaScript that adds optional static typing. This feature is crucial for larger codebases, as it helps catch bugs during development rather than at runtime. In this chapter, we will explore how to structure a scalable front-end architecture using TypeScript, focusing on best practices and design patterns that promote maintainability and team collaboration.

10.2 Benefits of Using TypeScript

Static Typing: TypeScript allows developers to define types for variables, function parameters, and objects. This feature can prevent many common errors and improve code quality.

Enhanced Tooling: With TypeScript, developers gain access to improved code editors and tooling, which offer intelligent autocompletions, inline documentation, and refactoring capabilities.

Early Bug Detection: By defining types and interfaces,

developers can catch bugs early in the development process, reducing the number of runtime exceptions.

Interoperability: TypeScript is fully compatible with JavaScript. Developers can gradually adopt it within existing projects, ensuring that they can leverage TypeScript's advantages without a complete rewrite.

10.3 Architectural Patterns for Scaling Front-End Applications

Building a scalable architecture requires understanding certain design principles and patterns. Here are some established architectural patterns suited for TypeScript applications:

10.3.1 Component-Based Architecture

In modern front-end development, particularly with frameworks like React and Vue, adopting a component-based approach is essential. This pattern breaks down the UI into reusable and encapsulated components, allowing for:

Reusability: Components can be reused across different parts of the application.

Isolation: Each component can manage its state and behavior, reducing the complexity of the application.

Simplified Testing: Isolated components can be tested independently, making unit tests straightforward.

When using TypeScript, defining props and state as interfaces within each component provides clarity and type safety:

```typescript
```

```typescript
interface ButtonProps { label: string;
onClick: () => void;
}
const Button: React.FC<ButtonProps> = ({ label, onClick
}) => { return <button
onClick={onClick}>{label}</button>;
};
```

10.3.2 Service Layer Architecture

In a scalable application, separating business logic from UI concerns is critical. This separation can be achieved through a service layer, which manages API calls, data manipulation, and caching.

Single Responsibility: Services handle specific tasks, which keeps components focused solely on rendering.

Easier Testing: Service logic can be tested independently from UI components. A typical service might look like this:

```typescript
interface ApiResponse<T> { data: T;
error?: string;
}
class UserService {
private readonly apiUrl = 'https://api.example.com/users';
async getUser(userId: string): Promise<ApiResponse<User>> { const response = await
```

```
fetch(`${this.apiUrl}/${userId}`);
if (!response.ok) {
return { data: null, error: 'User not found' };
}
const user: User = await response.json(); return { data:
user };
}
}
```
```

#### 10.3.3 State Management

As applications scale, managing state becomes increasingly difficult. Utilizing a predictable state management library, such as Redux or MobX, can greatly aid in maintaining a consistent application state.

**Centralized State**: A single source of truth for application state can simplify data flow and debugging.

**Type Safety**: By defining action types and state shapes with TypeScript, the application can ensure data integrity.

Here's an example of defining a Redux action and its type:

```typescript
interface FetchUserAction { type: 'FETCH_USER';
payload: User;
}

const fetchUser = (user: User): FetchUserAction => ({
```

174
```

```
type: 'FETCH_USER',
payload: user,
});
```

10.4 Following Best Practices

To ensure a scalable TypeScript architecture, developers should adopt certain best practices:

Project Structure: Maintain a clear folder structure that separates components, services, models, and utilities. A preferred structure could look like:

```
src/
```

components/ services/ models/ hooks/

utils/

```
```

Use of Types and Interfaces: Utilize TypeScript's ability to define types and interfaces thoroughly across your application to enhance clarity.

Consistent Naming Conventions: Maintain consistent naming conventions for files, functions, and variables. Use camelCase for functions and variables, and PascalCase for component names.

Error Handling: Implement robust error handling mechanisms to manage unexpected issues while keeping the user experience in mind.

Documentation: Maintain clear documentation, including comments in the code, to guide team members through the architecture and logic.

A scalable front-end architecture using TypeScript can significantly improve a development team's ability to create complex applications. By leveraging TypeScript's powerful typing system and methodologies like component-based design, service layers, and state management, developers can build applications that are not only usable but also maintainable and easy to extend over time.

Organizing TypeScript Projects for Maintainability and Scalability

TypeScript, with its strong typing and enhanced tooling features, is becoming increasingly popular for large- scale applications. However, simply using TypeScript does not guarantee a maintainable and scalable codebase. Clearly structured and organized projects are essential. This chapter explores best practices for organizing TypeScript projects to achieve maintainability and scalability.

1. Project Structure

A well-thought-out directory structure is the cornerstone of any maintainable codebase. For TypeScript projects, consider adopting a modular structure where files are organized based on functionality rather than the type of file (e.g., components, services, utilities). Here's a general outline of a scalable project structure:

```
`  `
```

/src

/components

```
/services
/hooks
/utils
/models
/views
/styles
/tests
/config index.ts App.tsx
```
```

### Components

In the `/components` folder, store all reusable UI components. Each component should be in its own folder, containing related styles, tests, and potentially a README file. This modular way of organizing allows developers to understand and locate components easily.

### Services

The `/services` directory can hold all logic related to API calls, database interactions, and other business logic. Organizing services this way promotes separation of concerns, making your application easier to manage and update.

### Hooks

For applications using React, the `/hooks` directory should contain custom hooks. This encapsulation can promote code reuse and improve the readability of your components.

177
```

Utilities

The `/utils` folder should contain helper functions that can be reused across different parts of your application. Keeping utility functions organized also simplifies testing and debugging.

Models

In the `/models` directory, define TypeScript interfaces or types that clarify the shape of data throughout your application. Clear type definitions help maintain consistency and make it easier to refactor in the future.

Tests

As part of maintaining a robust codebase, tests should be in their own `/tests` folder or alongside the components they correspond to. Use a consistent naming convention for test files to simplify their identification.

Configuration

Store configuration files and environment variables in the `/config` directory. This approach helps in making environment-specific changes more manageable without affecting the core application logic.

2. Managing Dependencies

Dependencies play a critical role in project maintainability. Use package managers like npm or yarn to manage your dependencies. Identify core libraries and group third-party dependencies logically in the

`package.json` file. Performing regular updates and audits of your dependencies is crucial to avoid security vulnerabilities and keep your application running on the latest features.

3. Implementing Type Safety

TypeScript's main feature is its type system. Invest the time to define comprehensive types and interfaces. Use `strict` mode in your `tsconfig.json` file to enforce strict type-checking, enabling safer, more predictable code that is easier to maintain.

```json
{
"compilerOptions": { "strict": true,
// other configurations
}
}
```

Moreover, consider creating a types directory for custom types and third-party type definitions. This practice aids in preventing type-related issues, thereby reducing the need for refactoring.

4. Documentation and Comments

As your project grows, so does its complexity. Invest time in writing/documenting your code. Each component, function, and class should have clear comments explaining its purpose, parameters, and return types. Tools like TypeDoc can generate documentation from TypeScript comments, facilitating better understanding and maintenance.

5. Testing for Stability

Writing robust tests is an integral part of maintaining a

179

codebase. Utilize testing frameworks (like Jest or Mocha) and libraries (like React Testing Library) to write unit tests, integration tests, and end-to-end tests. A solid suite of tests allows changes to be implemented confidently and efficiently, ensuring that existing functionality remains intact.

6. Modularization and Code Splitting

Leverage techniques provided by TypeScript and your chosen framework (e.g., React's lazy loading features) to break your application into smaller, manageable pieces. This modular approach, sometimes referred to as code splitting, allows parts of your application to load only when needed, improving load times and overall performance.

7. Version Control

Use Git or another version control system to manage your project's development. Structured commits that follow a standardized format (like Conventional Commits) not only encourage clear history but also assist in automated version release processes.

8. CI/CD Setup

Implement a Continuous Integration/Continuous Deployment (CI/CD) pipeline to automate testing and deployment processes. Tools like GitHub Actions or Travis CI can help streamline these processes, ensuring that every change to the codebase undergoes testing and quality assurance before being deployed.

Emphasizing these practices not only eases the developer's journey but also enhances collaboration across teams, setting the stage for sustainable growth and evolution of the project in the long run. By investing in organization and best practices from the outset, you set your TypeScript project up for success in the ever- evolving tech landscape.

Implementing Modular, Reusable, and Type-Safe Front-End Code

Developers are increasingly turning to TypeScript, a superset of JavaScript, to help build maintainable, scalable, and efficient web applications. This chapter will delve into the best practices for implementing modular, reusable, and type-safe front-end code using TypeScript, allowing developers to streamline their workflow and ensure code quality.

1. Understanding TypeScript and Its Benefits

TypeScript provides a robust type system that can catch errors early during compile time, which is a significant improvement over JavaScript's dynamic typing. By introducing strong typing, TypeScript enhances code readability and maintainability, making it easier for teams to collaborate on large code bases. Key benefits include:

Early Error Detection: TypeScript catches errors before execution, reducing runtime issues.

Enhanced IntelliSense: IDEs provide better autocompletion and inline documentation due to type information.

Improved Code Structure: With interfaces, enums, and advanced types, developers can create better-structured code.

2. Modular Code Design

A modular approach to front-end development involves breaking down the application into smaller, self-contained units or modules. This architecture promotes reusability and separation of concerns.

2.1 Creating Modules

In TypeScript, you can define a module using either the ES6 module syntax or the CommonJS module syntax. ES6 modules are generally preferred for their simplicity and integration with modern JavaScript tooling.

```typescript
// mathUtils.ts

export function add(a: number, b: number): number {
return a + b;
}

export function subtract(a: number, b: number): number {
return a - b;
}
```

2.2 Importing and Using Modules

To use the created modules in other parts of your application, you can import them as follows:

```typescript
import { add, subtract } from './mathUtils';

const result = add(5, 10); console.log(result); // 15
```

2.3 Organizing Modules

Organizing your modules in a logical directory structure is crucial. Consider grouping related functionalities together and using index files to aggregate exports:

```
/utils mathUtils.ts stringUtils.ts index.ts
```

The `index.ts` file can re-export everything:

```typescript
// index.ts
export * from './mathUtils'; export * from './stringUtils';
```

3. Reusable Components

Component-based architecture is at the core of modern front-end development. Libraries like React and Vue embrace this paradigm, allowing developers to create components that can be reused across applications.

3.1 Defining Reusable Components

In TypeScript, defining a reusable component involves specifying props with appropriate types:

```tsx
import React from 'react';

interface ButtonProps { label: string;

onClick: () => void;

}
```

183

```tsx
const Button: React.FC<ButtonProps> = ({ label, onClick
}) => { return <button
onClick={onClick}>{label}</button>;
};

export default Button;
```

3.2 Leveraging Generics

Generics allow you to build reusable components that work with a variety of types. This is particularly useful when dealing with user input or forms:

```tsx
interface InputProps<T> {

value: T;

onChange: (value: T) => void;

}

const Input = <T extends unknown>({ value, onChange }: InputProps<T>) => {

return <input value={value as string} onChange={(e) => onChange(e.target.value as unknown as T)} />;

};
```

3.3 Styling Reusable Components

To maintain consistency in styling, consider using CSS Modules or a system like styled-components. This encapsulates styles and prevents conflicts in larger applications.

4. Ensuring Type Safety

Type safety is one of the standout features of TypeScript, and it's essential for maintaining good code quality.

4.1 Defining Types and Interfaces

Utilize interfaces and type aliases to define the shape of your data. This enhances the self-documenting nature of the code:

```typescript
interface User {
id: number; name: string; email: string;
}
function getUser(id: number): User {
// Implementation goes here
}
```

4.2 Using Enums for Fixed Values

When dealing with a fixed set of values, enums provide a clear and concise way to handle them:

```typescript
enum UserRole {
Admin, User, Guest,
}
function checkAccess(role: UserRole) {
// Logic for checking access
}
```

4.3 Type Guards and Utility Types

Type guards enable you to create functions that narrow down types, while utility types like `Partial`, `Pick`, and `Record` can greatly simplify type manipulations and enhance code readability.

```typescript
function isAdmin(user: User): user is User & { role:
UserRole.Admin } { return user.role ===
UserRole.Admin;
}
```

5. Tools and Practices

To implement modular, reusable, and type-safe code effectively, consider leveraging the following tools and practices:

TypeScript Compiler: Always run the TypeScript compiler to check for type errors before deployment.

ESLint with TypeScript: Enforce coding standards and best practices using ESLint configured for TypeScript.

Prettier: Automatically format your code to maintain a clean and readable style.

Unit Testing: Write unit tests for your components using frameworks like Jest to ensure they work as expected.

By leveraging TypeScript's capabilities, developers can create applications that are easier to maintain, less prone to bugs, and more resilient to change. In this chapter, we've explored how to structure your TypeScript code

186

effectively, create reusable components, and ensure type
safety.

Chapter 11: Type-Safe State Management

In this chapter, we will explore how to implement type-safe state management in TypeScript, ensuring that our application state is both reliable and maintainable. We'll delve into various patterns and libraries, including how to use TypeScript's features to enhance the robustness of our state management solutions.

11.1 Understanding State Management

Before diving into the implementation, let's clarify what state management entails. In the context of web applications, "state" refers to the data that dictates the behavior and appearance of your app at any given time. This can encompass UI states, user authentication, fetched data, form inputs, and more. Effective state management helps in:

Maintaining Consistency: Ensuring that the UI remains in sync with the underlying data.

Enabling Predictability: Facilitating a clear flow of data and events, which can be crucial for debugging and testing.

Encouraging Reusability: Allowing components to be more easily reused across different parts of the application.

11.2 Why Type Safety Matters

Type safety is a feature of TypeScript that ensures the type correctness of variables, function parameters, and return types at compile time. This eliminates a whole class of runtime errors, leading to code that is easier to reason about, refactor, and maintain. When managing state, type safety enables:

Error Prevention: Type errors can be caught early during development.

Better Developer Experience: With IDE support for type definitions, developers benefit from autocompletion and inline documentation.

Enhanced Code Documentation: Type annotations serve as documentation for component interfaces and expected data shapes, improving collaboration among team members.

11.3 Basic Type-Safe State Management

Let us start by flattening state management using a simple example of a counter application.

```typescript
typescript type State = { count: number;
};
enum ActionType { INCREMENT = 'INCREMENT',
DECREMENT = 'DECREMENT',
}
type Action =
| { type: ActionType.INCREMENT }
| { type: ActionType.DECREMENT }; const initialState:
State = { count: 0 };
```

```typescript
function reducer(state: State, action: Action): State {
switch (action.type) {

case ActionType.INCREMENT: return { count: state.count
+ 1 }; case ActionType.DECREMENT: return { count:
state.count - 1 }; default:

return state;

}

}
```

In this simple setup:

We define a `State` type to describe what our state looks
like.

An `ActionType` enum provides a set of possible actions,
enhancing clarity and preventing typos.

The `Action` type union describes the different actions
that can be dispatched.

The `reducer` function handles the logic of transitioning
from one state to another based on the dispatched action.

11.3.1 Using useReducer Hook

In a React application, we can leverage the `useReducer`
hook to manage the state.

```typescript
import React, { useReducer } from 'react';

const Counter: React.FC = () => {

const [state, dispatch] = useReducer(reducer, initialState);

return (
```

```
<div>
<p>Current Count: {state.count}</p>
<button onClick={() => dispatch({ type:
ActionType.INCREMENT })}>Increment</button>
<button onClick={() => dispatch({ type:
ActionType.DECREMENT })}>Decrement</button>
</div>
);
};
export default Counter;
```

Here, the `Counter` component utilizes the `useReducer`
for state management, ensuring that both the state and
actions are type-safe.

11.4 Advanced State Management: Redux with
TypeScript

While the `useReducer` hook is great for local state
management, many applications require a more
centralized state management solution. Redux is a popular
choice for this purpose. Let's explore how to integrate
Redux with TypeScript.

11.4.1 Setting Up Redux Install Redux and its types:

```bash
npm install redux react-redux @types/react-redux
```

Define the state and actions in a similar way as before:

```typescript
// store.ts
import { createStore } from 'redux';
type ReduxState = { count: number;
};
const initialState: ReduxState = { count: 0 };
const COUNT_INCREMENT = 'COUNT_INCREMENT';
const COUNT_DECREMENT = 'COUNT_DECREMENT';
type Action =
| { type: typeof COUNT_INCREMENT }
| { type: typeof COUNT_DECREMENT };
const reducer = (state: ReduxState = initialState, action:
Action): ReduxState => { switch (action.type) {
case COUNT_INCREMENT:
return { ...state, count: state.count + 1 }; case
COUNT_DECREMENT:
return { ...state, count: state.count - 1 }; default:
return state;
}
};
const store = createStore(reducer);
export { store, Action, ReduxState,
COUNT_INCREMENT, COUNT_DECREMENT };
```

```
```

11.4.2 Using Redux in a Component

Connect your components to the Redux store using the `useSelector` and `useDispatch` hooks.

```typescript
import React from 'react';

import { useSelector, useDispatch } from 'react-redux';

import { ReduxState, COUNT_INCREMENT, COUNT_DECREMENT } from './store';

const Counter: React.FC = () => {

const count = useSelector((state: ReduxState) => state.count); const dispatch = useDispatch();

return (

<div>

<p>Current Count: {count}</p>

<button onClick={() => dispatch({ type: COUNT_INCREMENT })}>Increment</button>

<button onClick={() => dispatch({ type: COUNT_DECREMENT })}>Decrement</button>

</div>

);

};

export default Counter;
```
```

In this example, the `useSelector` hook pulls the current

193
```

count from the Redux state, while `useDispatch` sends actions to the store. Type safety is maintained throughout the flow thanks to TypeScript.

11.5 Leveraging Middleware for Side Effects

In more complex applications, you may encounter side effects such as API calls. Here, middleware like Redux Thunk or Redux Saga can be very helpful.

11.5.1 Using Redux Thunk

To implement async actions with Redux Thunk while maintaining type safety, follow these steps:

Install Redux Thunk:

```bash
npm install redux-thunk @types/redux-thunk
```

Extend the `Action` and use Thunk in your action creators:

```typescript
import { ThunkAction } from 'redux-thunk'; import { RootState } from './rootReducer';

type ThunkResult<R> = ThunkAction<R, RootState, unknown, Action>; const fetchData = (): ThunkResult<void> => async (dispatch, getState) => {
```

// Perform async operations

```
const response = await fetch('/api/data'); const data = await response.json();
```

```
dispatch({ type: 'SET_DATA', payload: data });
};
```
```

Type-safe state management is a powerful paradigm in TypeScript applications. By defining explicit types for state and actions, we can leverage TypeScript's capabilities to create more robust, maintainable, and understandable code. Whether you choose to use local state management through hooks or centralized management with libraries like Redux, the principles of type safety remain paramount.

With a firm foundation in type-safe state management, you are now equipped to tackle complex application challenges while minimizing bugs and improving the overall developer experience.

# Using Redux, Zustand, and Jotai with TypeScript

Among numerous state management libraries available, Redux, Zustand, and Jotai stand out with unique approaches, especially when utilized alongside TypeScript. In this chapter, we will explore these libraries, examine their strengths, and demonstrate how to integrate them with TypeScript for type safety and enhanced developer experience.

## 1. Introduction to State Management

State management is the practice of handling the state of an application in a predictable and efficient manner. In a React application, state represents the dynamic data that influences the rendering of components. As applications
```

grow in complexity, coordinating state across multiple components can become challenging.

Libraries like Redux, Zustand, and Jotai provide solutions to these problems, allowing developers to manage state in a centralized way.

1.1 Overview of Redux

Redux is one of the most popular state management libraries for JavaScript applications. It follows a unidirectional data flow, making it predictable and easier to debug. State in Redux is stored in a single object called the store, which can only be modified by dispatching actions that are handled by pure functions called reducers.

1.2 Overview of Zustand

Zustand is a smaller, more lightweight alternative to Redux. It provides a minimalistic API that simplifies state management without losing the core features developers need. Zustand allows for more localized state management and is often praised for its simplicity and performance.

1.3 Overview of Jotai

Jotai takes a different approach by using atoms to manage state. Each atom represents a piece of state, and components that use the atoms will re-render when the state changes. This granularity makes Jotai a flexible option for state management, especially in larger applications where different components may need to subscribe to different states.

2. Setting Up the Environment

To get started, ensure you have a React project set up with TypeScript. You can create a new project using Create

React App:
```bash
npx create-react-app my-app --template typescript cd my-app
```

Install the required libraries:
```bash
npm install redux react-redux zustand jotai
```

3. Using Redux with TypeScript ### 3.1 Setting Up Redux

To use Redux with TypeScript, we'll create a simple counter application. #### 3.1.1 Defining Types

Define your state and action types:
```typescript
// types.ts
export interface CounterState { count: number;
}
export const INCREMENT = "INCREMENT"; export const DECREMENT = "DECREMENT";
interface IncrementAction { type: typeof INCREMENT;
}
interface DecrementAction { type: typeof DECREMENT;
}
```

```typescript
export type CounterActionTypes = IncrementAction |
DecrementAction;
```

3.1.2 Creating the Reducer

Next, create a reducer to manage the counter state:

```typescript
// reducer.ts
import { CounterState, CounterActionTypes,
INCREMENT, DECREMENT } from './types';

const initialState: CounterState = { count: 0,
};

export const counterReducer = (state = initialState,
action: CounterActionTypes): CounterState => { switch
(action.type) {
case INCREMENT:
return { count: state.count + 1 }; case DECREMENT:
return { count: state.count - 1 }; default:
return state;
}
};
```

3.1.3 Configuring the Store Create a store using Redux:

```typescript
// store.ts
```

```typescript
import { createStore } from 'redux';
import { counterReducer } from './reducer';
const store = createStore(counterReducer); export default store;
```

3.1.4 Connecting Redux to React

Finally, connect your Redux store to the application:

```typescript
// index.tsx
import React from 'react';
import ReactDOM from 'react-dom'; import { Provider } from 'react-redux'; import App from './App';
import store from './store';
ReactDOM.render(
<Provider store={store}>
<App ></App>
</Provider>, document.getElementById('root')
);
```

3.1.5 Creating Components

Create a counter component that uses Redux state:

```typescript
// Counter.tsx
import React from 'react';
```

```typescript
import { useSelector, useDispatch } from 'react-redux';
import { INCREMENT, DECREMENT } from './types';
import { CounterState } from './types';

const Counter = () => {

const count = useSelector((state: CounterState) =>
state.count); const dispatch = useDispatch();

return (

<div>

<h1>{count}</h1>

<button onClick={() => dispatch({ type: INCREMENT
})}>Increment</button>

<button onClick={() => dispatch({ type: DECREMENT
})}>Decrement</button>


</div>
);
};

export default Counter;
```

4. Using Zustand with TypeScript

Zustand's API is incredibly straightforward, making it a favorite for many developers. ### 4.1 Defining State

Create a Zustand store for the counter:

```typescript
// store.ts
```

```typescript
import create from 'zustand';
interface StoreState { count: number; increment: () =>
void; decrement: () => void;
}
const useStore = create<StoreState>((set) => ({ count: 0,
increment: () => set((state) => ({ count: state.count + 1
})), decrement: () => set((state) => ({ count: state.count -
1 })),
}));
export default useStore;
```

4.2 Creating Components

Create a counter component that uses Zustand state:

```typescript
// Counter.tsx
import React from 'react'; import useStore from './store';
const Counter = () => {
const count = useStore((state) => state.count);
const increment = useStore((state) => state.increment);
const decrement = useStore((state) => state.decrement);
return (
<div>
<h1>{count}</h1>
<button onClick={increment}>Increment</button>
```

```tsx
      <button onClick={decrement}>Decrement</button>
    </div>
  );
};
export default Counter;
```

5. Using Jotai with TypeScript

Jotai's atom-based approach provides fine-grained reactivity, which can be advantageous in complex applications.

5.1 Defining Atoms Create an atom for our counter:

```typescript
// atoms.ts
import { atom } from 'jotai';
export const countAtom = atom(0);
```

5.2 Creating Components

Create a counter component that uses Jotai:

```typescript
// Counter.tsx
import React from 'react'; import { useAtom } from 'jotai';
import { countAtom } from './atoms';
const Counter = () => {
const [count, setCount] = useAtom(countAtom);
```

```jsx
  return (
    <div>
      <h1>{count}</h1>
      <button onClick={() => setCount((c) => c + 1)}>Increment</button>
      <button onClick={() => setCount((c) => c - 1)}>Decrement</button>
    </div>
  );
};

export default Counter;
```

Choosing the right state management library depends on the specific needs of a project and personal preference. Redux, Zustand, and Jotai each have their strengths that suit different scenarios.

Redux is excellent for large-scale applications requiring complex state management, providing a structured way to manage application state.

Zustand offers a minimalist and lightweight approach, suitable for simpler applications that still require efficient state management.

Jotai is ideal for applications needing fine-grained control over reactivity with its atom-based model.

Best Practices for Global State Management in TypeScript-Based Apps

This chapter will explore best practices for global state management in TypeScript-based applications, ensuring that data flows consistently and changes are predictable. We will delve into various state management libraries, patterns, and techniques that can enhance your application's architecture, making it more efficient and easier to maintain.

1. Understanding Global State Management

Global state refers to data that needs to be accessed or manipulated across different parts of an application. Typical examples include user authentication status, cart items in e-commerce applications, and global settings or configurations. Managing this state effectively is crucial for a smooth user experience.

1.1 The Need for State Management

In smaller applications, passing state through props may suffice. However, as applications scale, prop drilling becomes cumbersome and error-prone. Effective global state management ensures that:

State can be accessed and modified from anywhere in the application.

The application remains performant, even when state changes frequently.

The flow of data is predictable and easier to debug. ## 2. Choosing the Right State Management Library

There is a plethora of state management libraries available for TypeScript applications. Selecting the right one largely depends on your specific requirements, team expertise, and the scale of your application.

Commonly used libraries include:

Redux: A popular choice for larger applications, offering a predictable state container.

MobX: Provides observability and allows for more straightforward handling of state with less boilerplate.

React Query: Suitable for data-fetching scenarios, focusing on server state management.

Zustand: A minimalist approach to state management that is easy to integrate and provides a simple API.

2.1 Criteria for Selection

When choosing a library, consider the following factors:

Learning Curve: Assess how easy it is for your team to adopt the library.

TypeScript Support: Ensure that the library provides complete type definitions and an easy way to use TypeScript types.

Community and Ecosystem: Libraries with a larger community often have better support, more tutorials, and a rich ecosystem of middleware and tools.

3. Structuring the Global State

A well-structured global state is key to managing complexity. Define a clear state shape and break it down into manageable slices, each responsible for a specific piece of data. This modularity makes maintenance easier and reduces cognitive load.

3.1 Defining Types and Interfaces

In TypeScript, leverage interfaces and types to define the shape of your global state clearly. For example:

```typescript
typescript interface User { id: string; name: string; email: string;
}

interface AppState { user: User | null; cartItems: string[]; isLoading: boolean;
}

const initialState: AppState = { user: null,

cartItems: [], isLoading: false,

};
```

Your state's structure should mirror the application's requirements and reflect its hierarchy logically. ## 4. Managing Side Effects

Handling side effects (like API calls) is often where complexity can escalate. It's important to clearly separate state management from side effects to maintain clean and testable code.

4.1 Utilizing Middleware

In Redux, for instance, you can use middleware such as Redux Thunk or Redux Saga to handle asynchronous actions. With TypeScript, ensure that your action creators are correctly typed to maintain type safety.

Example using Redux Thunk:

```typescript
export const fetchUser = (userId: string):
ThunkAction<void, AppState, unknown, Action<string>>
=> async dispatch => {
dispatch({ type: 'FETCH_USER_REQUEST' });

try {
const response = await fetch(`/api/user/${userId}`);
const user: User = await response.json();
dispatch({ type: 'FETCH_USER_SUCCESS', payload: user });
} catch (error) {
dispatch({ type: 'FETCH_USER_FAILURE', error });
}
};
```

4.2 Leveraging Async/Await

Using `async/await` can simplify your logic, making your code cleaner and easier to read. The TypeScript compiler can catch common errors during development, further reducing potential runtime issues.

5. Enhancing Performance with Memoization

As state changes, re-rendering components can lead to performance bottlenecks. Use memoization techniques to prevent unnecessary renders by leveraging React's `memo`, `useMemo`, and `useCallback` hooks effectively.

5.1 Example of Memoization

```typescript
const CartComponent: React.FC<{ items: CartItem[] }> =
memo(({ items }) => { return (
<div>
{items.map(item => (
<CartItem key={item.id} {...item} ></CartItem>
))}
</div>
);
});
```

By memoizing the `CartComponent`, it will only re-render when `items` change, improving performance. ## 6. Testing Your State Management

Robust testing of your state management ensures reliability and helps prevent regressions. Use TypeScript's type-checking alongside libraries like Jest or React Testing Library to create comprehensive unit and integration tests.

6.1 Testing Reducers and Actions

When testing Redux reducers, ensure that they return the expected state given certain actions:

```typescript
import reducer from './reducer';
```

```
test('should handle FETCH_USER_SUCCESS', () => {
const initialState = { user: null };

const action = { type: 'FETCH_USER_SUCCESS',
payload: { id: '1', name: 'John' } }; const newState =
reducer(initialState, action);


expect(newState.user).toEqual(action.payload);
});
```
` ` `

By leveraging TypeScript's features and following best practices in structuring state, managing side effects, enhancing performance, and thorough testing, you can create applications that are not only performant but also easier to understand and evolve over time.

Conclusion

As we reach the end of our journey through "TypeScript for Front End Development: Reduce Errors, Boost Productivity, and Master Modern Web Development Like a Pro," it's clear that TypeScript is not just a tool but an essential companion for any front-end developer dedicated to delivering high-quality web experiences.

Throughout this book, we've explored the myriad benefits of TypeScript, from its static typing that significantly reduces errors to its robust features that enhance productivity and maintainability. You've learned how to effectively integrate TypeScript into your development workflow, write clean and scalable code, and leverage powerful tools that the TypeScript ecosystem offers.

We have discussed various real-world applications and practical examples that demonstrate how TypeScript can streamline the development process, foster collaboration within teams, and ultimately lead to more reliable and performant applications. By investing time to master TypeScript, you're not just learning a new language, but you're equipping yourself with the skills to tackle complex web development challenges with confidence and clarity.

As you continue your development journey, keep in mind the importance of continuous learning and adaptation. The web development landscape is ever-evolving, and staying updated with new features, community practices, and tools will ensure that you remain at the forefront of the industry.

We encourage you to experiment with TypeScript in your projects, contribute to the growing community, and explore additional resources to deepen your understanding. The skills you develop with TypeScript will not only enhance your current projects but also open doors to future opportunities in modern web development.

Thank you for taking the time to read this book. We hope you feel empowered to harness the full potential of TypeScript and to create web applications that are both robust and elegant. Remember, the path to becoming a proficient developer requires practice, patience, and a passion for learning, so keep coding, keep exploring, and enjoy the rich possibilities that TypeScript and modern web development have to offer!

Biography

Adriam is a passionate innovator and a visionary in the world of **Miller**, blending deep expertise with a relentless drive to push boundaries. With a background rooted in **web development, TypeScript programming, and blockchain technology**, Adrian thrives at the intersection of cutting-edge technology and practical applications. His work in **web applications** has empowered countless developers and entrepreneurs to build scalable, high-performance digital solutions.

Beyond his technical prowess, Adrian is fueled by a love for problem-solving and creative innovation. Whether he's architecting blockchain solutions or refining his latest **TypeScript-powered application**, his mission is always the same—to simplify the complex and unlock new possibilities for others.

When he's not coding or writing, you'll find Adrian exploring the ever-evolving landscape of decentralized technology, mentoring aspiring developers, or experimenting with the latest web frameworks. His dedication to learning and sharing knowledge makes his work not just insightful but transformative.

Through this eBook, Adrian brings his expertise, passion, and real-world experience to guide readers on their own journey—offering not just knowledge, but a roadmap to success.

Glossary: Typescript for Front End Development

A

Abstract Class: A class that cannot be instantiated directly, and is meant to be subclassed. Abstract classes can contain abstract methods that must be implemented in derived classes.

Access Modifiers: Keywords in TypeScript (`public`, `private`, `protected`) that control the visibility and accessibility of class members.

B

Boxed Types: In TypeScript, boxed types refer to instances of objects wrapped around primitive data types, providing additional functionalities like methods and properties.

Built-in Types: Types that are natively supported by TypeScript, including `string`, `number`, `boolean`, `void`, `null`, and `undefined`. ### C

Class: A blueprint for creating objects with specific properties and methods. TypeScript extends JavaScript's class syntax by allowing type annotations and access modifiers.

Compiler: The TypeScript Compiler (tsc) transforms TypeScript code into plain JavaScript, checking for type errors and enabling features not found in older JavaScript versions.

Decorator: A special kind of declaration that can be attached to a class, method, accessor, property, or parameter, modifying its behavior. Decorators are experimental in TypeScript and enable powerful design patterns.

D

Dependency Injection (DI): A design pattern that allows a class to receive its dependencies from an external source rather than creating them internally, promoting loose coupling.

E

Enum: A way to define a set of named constants. Enums provide a convenient way to work with collections of related values in a type-safe manner.

Error Handling: The mechanism for responding to runtime errors in TypeScript applications, typically involving `try...catch` blocks, throwing exceptions, or handling promises.

F

Function Overloading: The ability to define multiple functions with the same name but different parameters. TypeScript allows overloading based on the types and numbers of arguments.

Generic Types: A way to create reusable components that can work with any data type while retaining type safety. Generics are denoted using angle brackets (e.g., `Array<T>`).

I

Interface: A structural type that defines a contract for classes, specifying the properties and methods that must be implemented. Interfaces are a powerful way to enforce type checks.

Intersection Types: A type that combines multiple types into one. An intersection type can contain all the members of the constituent types.

J

JavaScript: The programming language that TypeScript is based on. TypeScript extends JavaScript's capabilities by adding static typing and modern language features.

L

Literal Types: Specific types that allow you to express the exact value that a variable can hold. For example, `const direction: "left" | "right" = "left";` restricts `direction` to only two possible string values.

N

Namespace: A way to logically group related functionalities in TypeScript, helping to avoid naming conflicts by encapsulating code within a defined scope.

O

Object Type: A type that describes a non-primitive data type in TypeScript, defined by the properties it has, such as `{ name: string; age: number; }`.

Optional Parameters: Function parameters that can be omitted when calling the function, denoted by a question mark (e.g., `function greet(name?: string)`).

P

Promise: A built-in object in JavaScript (and consequently in TypeScript) used for asynchronous programming, representing a value that may be available now, or in the future, or never.

Type Assertion: A way to tell the TypeScript compiler

to treat a variable as a certain type without performing any special checking or restructuring of the variable. This can be done using the `as` syntax or by angle brackets (e.g., `let strLength: number = (str as string).length;`).

S

Static Typing: The ability to specify types at compile-time rather than run-time. This feature helps catch errors early in the development process.

Strict Mode: A way to opt into a restricted variant of JavaScript by enabling stricter parsing and error handling for your TypeScript code.

T

Tuple: An array with a fixed number of elements, where each element can have a different type. For example, a tuple of `[number, string]` can represent a pair of a number and a string.

Type Inference: The ability of TypeScript to automatically deduce the type of a variable based on its value or the context it is used in.

Type Union: A type that allows a variable to hold multiple types, denoted using the pipe (|) operator (e.g., `string | number`).

U

Union Type: A type that can be any one of several types. Union types are created by separating the types with a pipe (`|`).

V

Void: A type that indicates the absence of a value, often used as the return type of functions that do not return a value.

www.ingramcontent.com/pod-product-compliance
Lightning Source LLC
Chambersburg PA
CBHW070944050326
40689CB00014B/3337